"In the more than thirty years that I have collaborated, on and off, with Grandmother Spider, I have found her to be sincere and devoted in her work to create a healthy environment for the enhancement of the quality of life of those in behalf of whom she works. She has generously and selflessly applied the wisdom of the various Indigenous elders that have shared with her to add to the sum total of the beauty referred to in ancestral songs and prayers. The present work is an exemplary part of that personal mission. It not only sets forth much of the wisdom that was passed down to her by her Native American teachers, but also demonstrates her ability to add to that powerful base of sacred knowledge from her own fount of inspiration."

Miguel Sobaoko Koromo Sague, Caney Indigenous Spiritual Circle

"Spider is a pioneer in the deepest sense of the word. She served as a profound spiritual catalyst for me personally 20 years ago. Now her VORTEX ENERGY work will reach many, offering a planetary survival manual to assist our evolution into Universal Humans so that we can participate in conscious-cocreation of a beautiful world—inwardly and outwardly. It is time for this book. And I think that we are finally ready!"

Victoria Hanchin, author, The Seer and The Sayer: Revelations of the New Earth.

"These Vortex exercises enhance your 5th Dimensional energy and truly awaken and expand your consciousness. Life is so much richer when you keep yourself balanced and use the Vortex to manifest Love, Peace and Healing."

Jeanine S., Vortex Energy workshop participant

"...Your book opened my awareness up to the vortexes that surround us everywhere. They are a place of change and transformation and I now see them everywhere I look. It taught me that we are energy beings as well as solid human beings. ... I do vortex energy work almost daily...The Vortex Energy work helps me flow better, and it lets me know that there is an intelligence to the Universe. Taking time to work with that force and give it thanks makes me more grateful and trusting. ... I do a Vortex chakra cleaning regularly. It helps me to connect with the energy world. I have come to trust the Universe through doing energy work."

Don Shelters, Cattaraugus, NY, Vortex Energy workshop participant

"Not knowing what to expect about the experience of Vortex, I was gratefully surprised. It has brought back my sense of being; I could not even meditate to try to bring myself comfort or relief. The weight that was lifted off my shoulders was huge. I saw many colors, and felt energy shift through and around my body. The dark place I was in started to fill with the light I once remembered. The experience helped me more then any medication or therapy could. You have helped me very much... The Vortex work you do is a great gift that needs to be shared."

M.J., Vortex Energy healing client

VORTEX ENERGY

*Creating a Doorway for
Transformation & Evolution*

BALBOA
PRESS

A DIVISION OF HAY HOUSE

Balboa Press books may be ordered through booksellers or by contacting:

Balboa Press
A Division of Hay House
1663 Liberty Drive
Bloomington, IN 47403
www.balboapress.com
1 (877) 407-4847

Because of the dynamic nature of the Internet, any web addresses or links contained in this book may have changed since publication and may no longer be valid. The views expressed in this work are solely those of the author and do not necessarily reflect the views of the publisher, and the publisher hereby disclaims any responsibility for them.

The author of this book does not dispense medical advice or prescribe the use of any technique as a form of treatment for physical, emotional, or medical problems without the advice of a physician, either directly or indirectly. The intent of the author is only to offer information of a general nature to help you in your quest for emotional and spiritual well-being. In the event you use any of the information in this book for yourself, which is your constitutional right, the author and the publisher assume no responsibility for your actions.

Any people depicted in stock imagery provided by Thinkstock are models, and such images are being used for illustrative purposes only.
Certain stock imagery © Thinkstock.

ISBN: 978-1-4525-1592-2 (sc)
ISBN: 978-1-4525-1593-9 (e)

Library of Congress Control Number: 2014910004

Print information available on the last page.

Balboa Press rev. date: 04/16/2015

Vortex Energy

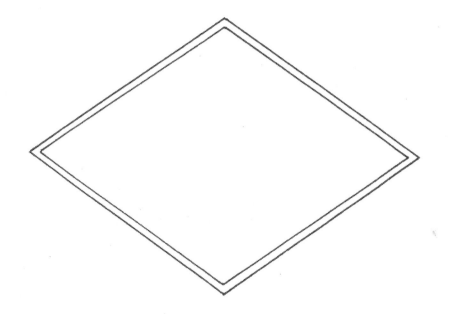

Creating a Doorway for
Transformation & Evolution

Spider is also the author of:

Songs of Bleeding–Taino women's ceremonies and passage rites, published by Black Thistle Press.

Katie's Journey–Moon Lodge Dreams–A contemporary young girl's passage rite ceremony.

Grandmother Spider and the Web of Life–The Medicine Wheel teachings of the Web of Life shield and story of Earth Changes.

All Our Relations–A children's story and activity book about the Medicine Wheel.

Taino Glyphs–Symbols that represent the Caney Circle Taino teachings with cards for readings.

Grandmothers of the Four Winds–A short story about the Medicine Wheel.

*Yet unpublished **Animal Teachers Cards for Kids**.

More information and excerpts from Spider's other works can be found on the website:

www.spidersmedicine.com

Vortex Energy

Creating a Doorway for Transformation & Evolution

I am grateful to the Star People from Lyre who shared these Vortex teachings and made sure I figured it all out. First and foremost, I honor my Elders and teachers of the Medicine Wheel for providing the Earth Connection. I am especially honored to be a part of the Caney Circle and work with Miguel Sague to help bring about the Reconciliation. I am grateful to have spent time with Seneca Grandmother Twylah Nitsch and the Peace Elders at the Wolf Clan Teaching Lodge. Thanks to my students these past 30 years who have shared their unique perspectives on the Vortex and the children who intuitively manifest the Vortex through their way of being. Much gratitude to Hollis Melton and Vikki Hanchin for their suggestions and advice. Many thanks to Tricia Drake and Jonathan Woolson for their support and assistance in preparing the manuscript to make this book possible. Finally, many thanks to Chelsie Kelley for her excellent design work that made the Vortex Energy workbook a reality.

The Star People shared the Vortex Energy information in this publication
to enable us to create a positive world that will benefit the evolution of
humans & all other species on this planet.

When we use Vortex Energy, we agree to the following two directives instructed by the Star People:

1. The Vortex is never used with intention.

2. When we work with the Vortex, we must also make a commitment to do Vortex Energy work for our planet because Vortex Energy work is meant to aid the evolution of Mother Earth as well as humans. It is not the intention of the Star People that we open our aware ness and leave this planet behind, but that we change our perspective and transform with her into the New World.

This book is dedicated to Katie Dolphin Bright Star and the other special Shining Children. *They will take us into the Arcs.*

Table of Contents

PART FOUR: VORTEX EXERCISES

PART FIVE: TIDBITS OF UNIVERSAL WISDOM

APPENDIX: ENERY ALIGNMENT WITH HEALING TRIANGLES

The Nature of Being

Multidimensional Reality

Like chords on a harp

Plucks an endless rhythm of energy

That resonates within the deepest layers of being

Reminding each of us

That our origins are stardust

Adrift in an ongoing dream

Manifesting life, love, truth, peace and wholeness

Out of chaos and darkness

Each energy chord a thought

Creating a stream of possibilities

Accented by its own emotion

As we experience the flow

Of joining together

The rhythm plays on

In a symphony of movement

Ever fluid, always changing

The many layers of being

Multidimensional Reality

We are
One Mind,
One Body,
One Heart,
And One Spirit,
Manifesting One Law
That holds together
The Dream of Creation.

Preface

My journey with the Vortex began during my first Vision Quest. Sitting in the Sacred Circle in my self-constructed vision quest hut, I spent four days singing and calling out to the Spirits to teach me what I needed to know to follow my spiritual path. On the third day, I was given a special gift. I looked down at my hands and saw a symbol glowing in both of my palms. I was told that this was my Medicine Symbol and it would bring strength and healing through working with my hands. I understood then that working with others—sharing healing through balancing energy vibrations—was an important aspect of my Medicine Path.

After this Vision Quest, I went on to become a Beike (Ceremony Leader) and Boitu (Ceremony Healer) with Miguel Sague and the Caney Indian Spiritual Circle, learning the Taino Medicine Wheel and working with other Beikes and Boitus to share the celebrations and ceremonies of the Taino tradition. My spiritual journey also took me to work with Grandmother Twylah Nitsch at the Wolf Clan Teaching Lodge where I spent years listening to Elders from many traditions speak about the story of Mother Earth and prophecies for the Earth Changes that were coming. During that time, I attended massage school and began to learn various hands-on healing modalities. While I pursued these interests, I continued wowrking with the Vortex symbol to gain a better understanding of how to use my gift.

About ten years later, my formal Vortex instruction began. One sunny late summer day, I walked with a friend to a park with the intention of doing a healing ceremony. However, once I started drumming, the park and healing ceremony vanished. I found myself in a field of beautiful luminous light. A sense of wholeness and perfection permeated this space; there was no separation between being and awareness.

I was not alone. Two other beings stood silently nearby and they wanted my attention. Much taller than any human, these beings were unlike any creature I could imagine. They seemed to glow from within. Their pale, luminous skin defined long legs with flat flipper-like feet. Their arms ended in hands with fingers more than twice as long as mine. Their gestures were subtle and enticing. But it was their eyes that really fascinated me. Taking up half of their triangular faces, their eyes were warm dark pools that drew me right in. Within this darkness it seemed the entire Universe existed.

An exchange happened between my awareness and their projections. Images and sounds touched my soul, conveying feelings, processes, and time spans. I saw myself as a traveler out of time and space watching the Universal Dream unfold, and instantly understanding many things about the Universal Plan for life. It became very clear how all beings on all worlds were intimately connected by a network of Energy Webs that intertwined and interconnected with each other, making the vast Universe one single energy being with many sensory centers.

Without speaking, through the Universal Language of the Heart, the beings then identified themselves as Star People from Lyre and told me that they were here to teach me how to use the Vortex symbol to align personal energy and assist with the evolution of the human species.

I understood the Star People to be multidimensional beings from somewhere out in the Lyre Constellation who traveled to this planet on a mission to benefit humans during our transition time. Many ancient cultures record through word and image similar Star People who have visited in the past to share with us. Some ancient cultures, I recalled, trace our human origins to the stars. I wondered if, within this grand network of Energy Webs, are these Star People our universal relations coming to remind us of the potential that we humans now have to evolve into Wholeness?

Much was communicated through all levels of my awareness. Finally, I was shown many geometric symbols and told how these symbols affect the flow of energy. They showed me how to use the Vortex, and then they showed me how the symbol could be used to attune planetary energy for the coming time of transformation. The same Vortex symbol that I have in my hands was then projected as a shining multidimensional form between their hands. I was aware that I was given this symbol, and that many others were given similar symbols, as keys to unlocking the Universal Wisdom and creative potential within the human species. I understood that we each were to individually work with our symbols, and then at the right time in our evolution, the symbols would be called to join together. When all the Vortex symbols are joined together, latent DNA codes will activate to manifest Wholeness.

A memory stirred from my distant past. I saw a shining ring of fire floating in the dark vastness of the Universe. Within the ring of fire were Completeness, Oneness, and Wholeness. It was the beginning place of all things, the matrix for the manifestation of the Dream of Living. As the fire flickered and glowed, I became aware that what I had thought was fire was actually light dancing to the vibration of creation. I was a part of this ring of fire. My vibrational light danced with the others. Together our energy began to shine brighter and brighter as we took the first steps of weaving the dream into reality. Each vibrational light embodied that shining energy. We became the Shining Ones.

A pulse went through the ring of fire. It was time. I felt myself volunteer to go and my vibrational light energy gently separated from the others. Immediately I missed the wholeness. I was aware of other vibrational light beings separating from the ring of fire and falling away. My vibrational light energy fell away and followed them. Soon the shining ring of fire was gone. Those of us that left became vibrational light energy stars shooting through the Universal Dream. I fell for what seemed an extraordinary long time past uncountable galaxies and star systems throughout the vast Universe. Finally, the darkness started to melt into a soft shade of blue. I kept falling, only slower, and now I was falling through a bright blue sky with light fluffy clouds. Down, down I fell until I could see the tops of green trees. The memory ended as my shining vibrational light being entered a physical body.

It is time, the Star People wordlessly reminded me. Awaken the Vortex that you carry. The Shining Ones are remembering why they are here. It is time for the Vortex symbols to come together to activate the DNA code of Wholeness.

I worked with the Vortex symbol for many years before I could fully understand the depth of this gift. The Star People visited me often during the first four years, showing me various ways to use the Vortex. A small group of students and friends helped me put the Vortex teachings into understandable terms so that it could be shared. Even now, after living with the Vortex symbol for more than thirty years, I discover new facets of Vortex Energy to explore and share. Through working with the Vortex, I have come to know that this symbol represents the totality of all that is; it is a visual representation of the song and dance of the Universe.

The Vortex is calling us home.

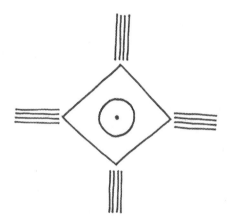

A Note to the Reader

Since the Vibrational Alignment in 1987, our planet has been going through major changes as Mother Earth shifts and moves, sending loud messages to her two-legged children to awaken. These messages are happening all around us every day with increasing intensity. Stressed out environmental resources are challenging the ways we live and work. Many animals and plants have become extinct or are on the verge of extinction. Landmasses are moving, seasons are shifting, and climate is changing. In every country, the government, economics and social systems are undergoing major changes. These Earth Changes are ushering in a new world and triggering the development of a new species of humans. The Great Planetary Doorway that opened during the time from the Winter Solstice of 2012 to the Summer Solstice of 2013 has changed the vibration of life. Things will never be the same.

We are now living in the Fifth World. Our way of thinking is being called to embrace a new vision of spiritual unity that includes equality for all life. Survival for our species depends on each one of us becoming aware of the Web of Life—the Energy Web that connects all beings. We must wake up and realize that every thought we have, every word we speak, and every action we offer reaches out to touch all life on this planet and beyond. We must remember who we are and why we are living at this crucial time. Dimensions are shifting, revealing potential way beyond anything that was available for our grandparents. It is up to each one of us to open up a clear energy channel and anchor this new multidimensional reality. We are the Creators.

This book is a survival manual written to share information about Vortex Energy, the term that the Star People use to describe these teachings of energy transformation. Vortex Energy is about actualizing universal awareness so that we, and our planet, can evolve using the most positive path to manifest the creative vibration of Unconditional Love. In sharing these Vortex Energy teachings, I explain how our personal energy is a reflection of our Earth Connection by using the Medicine Wheel. This works for me, as I am a teacher and ceremony leader in the Taino Caney Indian Spiritual Circle. However, the Vortex is not a religion or system of spiritual beliefs. It is a method of using personal, planetary and universal energy for healing and evolution. Each person who uses the Vortex can easily translate this healing energy within the context of their own spiritual understanding.

The Vortex has the intensity of an energy laser, thus clearing away blockages and rearranging both the energy and physical bodies. The vibration of Vortex Energy affects us on an intracellular level awakening latent DNA codes for evolution, on the physical level through re-generating tissues, on the emotional level transforming stress, and on the etheric level rearranging the situations and opportunities of our lives. Yet Vortex Energy goes beyond personal healing and strengthens our spiritual awareness with Universal Truth. Each time we use the Vortex, we assist our planetary evolution through reconnecting with all Energy Webs to create Wholeness. The vibration within the Vortex aligns our energy with all other life on this planet, aligns us with the vibration of the Earth itself, and aligns us with the other planets in our Universe and beyond. Vortex Energy work is multidimensional, enabling transformation of energy and awareness on many levels at the same time. The transformation of energy and awareness that happens within the Vortex manifests as healing within the physical body, emotional well being, harmonious relationships, and balance within the environment.

Some of the following information was published in 1991 as a workbook with the same title as this book. Since that time, I have expanded my use of Vortex Energy and have been led to share more Vortex teachings with those ready to work with them. This book is set up with instruction for beginners learning to use the Vortex. It is not necessary to have experience working with energy before learning to use the Vortex. The only requirement is a willingness to learn how to perceive energy and an open mind to translate what you find. Those who already use healing energy will find a different perspective when working with the Vortex. This information on Vortex Energy is meant to assist our planetary process of evolution into Wholeness. We are living in a New World with new energy vibrations, and the Vortex is one way that we can align our personal vibration with the changing energy.

We begin our Vortex journey with the Universal Energy Web and an overview of the Earth's Energy Web, including information on the evolution of our planet and how our personal Energy Webs interact with the planetary energy flow. Following are preparatory exercises and instruction on how to create a Vortex. Eighteen Vortex Energy exercises are included for aligning your own Energy Web and working with the Vortex for helping others align their Energy Webs. At the end, I have included an appendix on using Triangular Energy Configurations to align energy.

All of the information contained in this book has come from the Lyrians directly, brought in by Spider and a small group of friends working to remember how to use Vortex Energy to create our future. The instructions are written exactly as shared by the Star People. I am grateful for those special friends who listened to my thoughts and visions all these years, worked with the Vortex, and found their own paths to open the Vortex doorway. With this edition, I have changed some of the terms in an effort to make the Vortex Energy information more accessible for everyone. My apologies to the Vortex students who have worked with me over the years for any confusion that this may cause. Although you will find some different words, the original concepts and definitions remain the same.

We now live in the Fifth World where the use of I will become obsolete. For this reason, the point of view in this book is often written as first person plural. At this time, each individual must remember that we are individual physical manifestations of One Collective Energy Being. I refer to others as simply the person, or the plural they, in an effort to find a non-gender pronoun that reflects the existence of our Spirit Essence without the attachment of specific physical characteristics. We have left the Fourth World of Separation, and it is necessary to change our way of speaking to create new constructs that envision Wholeness. Although this way of speaking may appear awkward, as we refer to ourself as We, we program our energy to embody the awareness of the planetary consciousness of Wholeness. Also in this book you will find many words capitalized that may fall outside of the current definition of acceptable grammar. I have purposely capitalized words to call attention to special concepts and trigger an awakening of the Universal Wisdom of energy and creation that each one of us carries within.

During this time of Earth changes, we must begin to live accordingly. We are each called to return to the Sacred Tree to join in reconnecting the Web of Life. The dance of evolution quickens. A pulse flies through the Web, awakening awareness. We are One. We live, breathe and vibrate in harmony with Mother Earth, each other, and all other life. We are all Related. Let all of our thoughts, words and actions reflect this way of being. Let each of us become role models for our children. We are the parents of the new species, growing past the self-image of I to become We. We each have a piece of the puzzle. How exciting it is to see the pieces all come together to manifest the Fifth World!

I pass the message of the Star People along to you.

Remember.

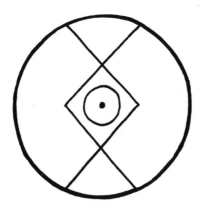

PART ONE: UNIVERSAL ENERGY WEBS

The Universe exists as a simplistic rhythm through which very complex forms have manifested. The basic forms of the Universe are geometric energy configurations that create the foundation for every living thing. It is time to remember the rhythm.

The Web of Life

If this book has caught your eye, you are most likely aware of an underlying energy that surrounds all beings and connects us forever. Each of our thoughts and actions go out to not only affect the intended recipient but, like ripples on a pond, the energy generated through our being and doing affects all other creatures, not only in our immediate environment but throughout the entire Universe. My Elders and teachers called this energy the Web of Life.

I was taught that each creature has a personal Energy Web that surrounds their Spirit Essence, connects them to their physical body and encloses their Sacred Space. When you came from the Spirit World, the only thing you brought into the Earth Walk was your Spirit Essence. Encoded within your Spirit Essence was the blueprint for this life, determined long before you were born, when you made your commitment for living. Your Spirit Essence is your seed of potential from the Great Mystery's dream and the piece of Universal Wisdom that you carry inside throughout your entire Earth Walk. Your Spirit Essence makes you unique among all of the other creatures that inhabit all of the worlds in this grand Universe.

Your personal Energy Web originates within your Vibrational Light Center, the energy center located just above your navel where your Spirit Essence resides. Your Energy Web connects your Spirit Essence with all aspects of your being. Going out from your Vibrational Light Center, your Energy Web weaves throughout your entire being, within and surrounding every tissue that makes up your physical body. From there, your Energy Web extends out and creates an electromagnetic energy space that surrounds your physical body. We call this Sacred Space because within your personal Energy Web you carry your feelings and thoughts, your purpose for living, and your gifts and abilities. The Sacred Space of your personal Energy Web surrounds everything that makes up who you are.

When you encounter another person, creature, or even a stone or plant, a strand of your Energy Web extends beyond the boundary of your Sacred Space to sense the energy of that other being. This happens very quickly, before you can speak or have time to notice the way that other being looks or the sounds it makes. Through that strand of energy, you know the vibration of that other being and can recognize if you are both in harmony. You can tell immediately if you will like that being or not. Through your energy strands, you may have a feeling of attraction, a strong unexplainable connection, or perhaps an uncomfortable feeling associated with that other being. Your Spirit Essence will feel this within your Vibrational Light Center. When you meet someone new, or feel uncomfortable around someone, always bring your awareness into your Vibrational Light Center and use your inner knowing. The feeling you get will guide your actions in the right direction.

It is possible to communicate through the strands of your Energy Web. No words are needed, just the sharing of feelings and vibrations. Our Ancestors communicated not only with each other but also with the animals, stones, plants and trees all around them. They found the best foods and medicines by following the inner feelings located within their Vibrational Light Center. This is how they spoke with and learned from the animals. Our energy strands, or Fine Lines as I call them in this book, communicate a complete understanding and awareness, unlimited in potential. Through these strands of our personal Energy Web, we each can exist in many dimensions.

This exercise is one way that we can experience a Fine Line connection to all of the other beings in the Web of Life. Find a natural, quiet place where you feel comfortable—such as by a pond, or next to a tree, or any outdoor place that feels special. Sit down on the ground and take a few deep breaths. Allow your energy to soften until you can feel the heartbeat of Mother Earth underneath you. Bring Mother Earth's heartbeat up inside your body and allow your own heartbeat to follow her rhythm. When you are comfortable, allow your energy to reach out and surround the pond, tree, or a nearby stone or plant. See if you can feel the vibration of this special being. Keep your thoughts focused on feeling this vibration and notice how it interacts with your vibrational light energy. Stay in this place awhile and just BE. When you feel ready, you can begin to ask questions to the other being. Ask through clear, focused thoughts. The answers you receive may be clear, but they may also come as feelings or vague perceptions that may take time to understand.

When you were born, you connected an energy strand, or Fine Line, to your mother that will remain intact throughout your entire life. Through this special connection, you can both tell what the other is thinking and can send love and special healing energy. Often times this energy strand is forgotten as babies grow older and energy perception is discouraged. However, it is not only possible but also natural to keep this connection open and use it often. As you get older, you find other people that resonate with your energy. These special people in your life share an energy strand, or Fine Line, with you and you can communicate on a deeper vibrational level with them.

During the birth process, you anchor Fine Lines within certain locations on the Earth. These places are your personal places of Earth Connection. That is why some people feel a familiarity with a country that they may never have visited. You may or may not consciously remember where your Fine Lines are anchored, but when you visit these locations you will feel it in your Spirit Essence and remember. Everyone—person, plant or creature—makes energy connections with special locations on the Earth. Your energy, and all of your thoughts and actions, is felt at each of your special locations, affecting the plants and creatures living there. Likewise, events occurring at each of your special locations can be felt in your personal Energy Web. In this respect, your personal health and well being is tied to the health and harmony of our planet. As we weave our personal Energy Webs, we strengthen the Planetary Energy Web.

When we are born, we also weave energy strands with a particular plant or tree that becomes our Medicine Plant and an animal that becomes our Guardian Spirit. If our Medicine Plant is a dandelion, we share a special energy connection with all dandelions that we come into contact with. Likewise, if our Guardian Spirit is a spider, we share a special energy connection with all spiders. Our Medicine Plant and Guardian Spirit remain closely connected to us throughout our entire life. If we develop a relationship with our Medicine Plant and Guardian Spirit, we always have access to guidance, healing and protection. For example, our Medicine Plant can be a good source of food or medicine when we need nourishment or healing, and our Guardian Spirit can be the voice of caution or lead us in making wise choices. In a similar way, we weave Fine Lines to connect with other worlds in this Universe so that we are personally aligned with them. These can be planets, suns or stars. If you feel attracted to a particular celestial body, you are experiencing the awareness of a Fine Line energy strand connection. What happens on those other worlds affects us through our Fine Lines, and likewise our thoughts and energy goes all the way out on the Universal Energy Web to reach these other Universal Worlds.

Indeed, the Web of Life is much more grand and complex than we could ever imagine. You can visualize the many Fine Line energy strands flowing out from your Energy Web and connecting with your special locations on the Earth—individual plants and trees—a creature being—your mother—special people in your life—and on out to other worlds in this vast Universe. Now imagine your Energy Web woven together with the energy strands of all the other people from every nation and all the stones, plants, trees, birds and creatures on the Earth. If we understand that an ecosystem survives as one complete living organism, with all of the species interdependent and necessary for the survival and growth of the entire ecosystem, then we must also know that within an ecosystem, the Energy Webs of all species are woven together into a singular Energy Web. The Energy Webs of different ecosystems are similarly woven together to make the Energy Web of a region or continent. Regional Energy Webs weave together as part of Mother Earth's Energy Web, which is a part of the Energy Web of our solar system. Our solar system weaves its Energy Web with the Energy Webs of all universal systems into the unity of the Great Energy Field of the Great Mystery.

Every planet, sun and star has a grand Energy Web that similarly weaves throughout its core and then reaches out to connect with all of the creatures living as part of that world. The Energy Web is the Sacred Space of each planet, sun and star. It carries all of the collective thoughts and feelings of the creatures that exist there, as well as the dream of life for that world, which is in turn a part of the Universal Dream of Living of the Great Mystery.

The Web of Life is so grand that all living things on all worlds are intricately bound up in its energy strands. The thoughts, feelings and actions of one individual being affect the entire Universal Energy Web. Changes that occur at the physical locations where your Energy Web is anchored directly affect your personal health and well being. What happens to one creature here on Earth affects the entire Web of Life all the way out to the ends of the Universe. Therefore, we have a responsibility to maintain the Web of Life with every one of our thoughts, feelings and actions. We depend on each other for survival more than we could ever imagine.

The Beginning

Everything that exists everywhere originated within the Universal Dream. Within the Dream World, forever before time existed, the Great Mystery that moves all things dreamed a long and very beautiful dream. The thought for life was conceived within the dream. This thought envisioned two worlds; the Spirit World where all spirit essence and potential exists, and the physical world where all possible forms can manifest and experience living.

Through the dream, the Great Mystery could experience every possible awareness in every dimension. The thought for life grew and became so expansive that it envisioned a myriad of life forms in many dimensions inhabiting many suns, stars and galaxies over vast reaches of infinite space. Each individual life form was intended to have a unique purpose and point of view. Each individual life form contributes equally to the dance of the dream unfolding, enabling the Great Mystery to experience All There Is. When all of the life forms on one world evolve to the point of merging together, that world will experience Wholeness. When all worlds experience Wholeness, the Universe will resonate once again as the Oneness of the Great Mystery. Thus, through the creation of life the Great Mystery experiences being on all levels, in every dimension, on every world.

This dream has been unfolding for many billions of years as each sun, star, planet, and each creature being that would inhabit all the dimensions, manifested in physical form and took their places in the Dream of Life. Each life form began as a thought; an energy that traveled throughout the Universe, gathering the necessary elements to create the physical form that would enable it to experience its part in the dream. As the thought energy grew, it created a grand Energy Web.

The Universe consists of millions of Energy Webs. Each thought envisioned in the Universal Dream went out and gathered energy to manifest a physical form, carrying with it the vibration, light, colors, sounds and an electromagnetic charge compatible with its specific form. These qualities surrounded the original thought and merged together to weave an Energy Web. Every person, creature, plant and tree, stone, planet, sun and star—indeed all things have an Energy Web. All Energy Webs shine with colors, light, and sound energy continually pulsing and glowing. They move together, connect and move away from each other, changing as they go. The never-ending dance of Energy Webs is the rhythm and light of life.

When you were still inside your mother preparing to enter the Earth Walk, Grandmother Spider wove your Energy Web around your physical body, anchoring your thought for being into physical form. Your Energy Web is attached to your physical body for the entire duration of your life. It is the place where the unseen exists. Thoughts, feelings and emotions are kept in your Energy Web, which then influence the growth and health of your physical body. What you think and feel today creates who you will become tomorrow. Your health, life situation and relationships are all a direct result of your prior thoughts.

Connections with others begin within your Energy Web when you send out Fine Lines to share energy before even exchanging words. You can choose to make special energy connections with people that you feel close to. You can also, consciously or unconsciously, take on the energy of another being through your Energy Web if you are not careful to keep the boundary of your Sacred

Space closed. Your Energy Web is anchored within the DNA in every cell in your body and has the power to heal and transform on a core level. The feelings and emotions that stay for a while in your Energy Web become encoded in your DNA and go on to affect your physical health if the DNA is not cleared of their energy. Feelings and emotions that become encoded within your DNA are eventually passed along to your children and their children, imprinting the entire human species.

As we walk upon the surface of Mother Earth, we interact with the Planetary Energy Web. Our individual Energy Webs overlap with that of the planet, as well as the creatures, plants, trees and stones in our vicinity. The energy that we share has a direct effect on all other life forms and their energy in turn influences us. Therefore, we are influenced by everything that we come into contact with. As the Energy Webs connect together, they overlap around the planet and then reach out to touch our neighbors in the Milky Way galaxy and beyond. The Universe is One Complete Energy Being, sharing the grand Universal Energy Web.

Since thoughts are light energy, we are all light. Positive thoughts let your light shine. The more you work with energy, the more your light will shine. Let your light shine!

The Matrix

The Universe is a grand force field consisting of infinite energy particles, most of which are too small for us to see. These energy particles exist in multiple dimensions that are well beyond our physical ability to observe. This force field, which our Native American Elders and other Aboriginal peoples referred to as the Great Mystery, is the matrix for all universal life. It motivated the creative process into being, which we call the Great Mystery's Dream, and is forever in a continual process of creativity. All Energy Webs are a part of this force field.

The Energy Matrix holds the essence of the Great Mystery's Dream. Like a pattern, the Energy Matrix triggers forms and events to unfold in accordance with the Great Mystery's Dream. Galaxies are born, planets solidify and become abundant with life, and beings exist on multiple dimensions, each following their specific purpose for living. Suns and stars burn out, beings pass from physical into spirit, planets transform and change. The Universe continually creates and renews itself in a harmonious dance of energy changing form.

Energy and dimensions are infinite. We can say that there are light energy vibrations and dense energy vibrations. Vibrations continue on indefinitely in all directions. For example, when you reach the highest or lightest energy that you can imagine, there is always another level of energy past that. Likewise, when you reach the lowest or most dense energy that you can imagine, there is always another level beyond that. Every dimension of existence contains both light and dense energy in a specific vibration that makes it unique. The Universe is in continual motion; expanding as far as it can go and then contracting back again to the center, each time creating a different circle of energy with different possibilities. The Web of Life moves the Energy Matrix in continual motion as the Dance of Living manifests all possible physical forms and creates all possible experiences in the richness of being in harmony with the Great Mystery.

Earth's Story

The story of planet Earth is one chapter of the universal story of energy manifesting into form. Earth's Energy Web reflects the thoughts of all beings living on the planet, which are then manifested as the environment around us. Thoughts are energy. In order for us to understand the Vortex, we need to know how the energy surrounding our planet developed and what changes we can expect now that we have entered the Fifth World.

The Earth has very long life cycles that we know of as Worlds. When the Earth has cycled through seven Worlds, her purpose will be complete. Many of us were born in the Fourth World, which ended on August 17, 1987. From August 17, 1987 until December 21, 2012, we lived in a transition period between the Fourth World and the Fifth World. It is evident everywhere that we are undergoing major personal and planetary changes. In order for us to prepare for the future, we must remember where we came from.

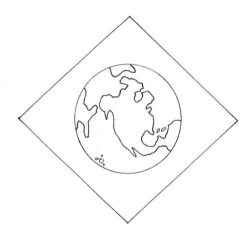

The First World—Thoughts manifesting Great Mystery's Dream

The First World

We are Spirit Beings who come from the Vibrational Light Center of the Universal Mind. We originated from a place of common thought awareness—the unity of the Great Energy Field. As Spirit Beings, we possessed a limited capacity to touch. Throughout the Great Energy Field, this limitation was felt and acknowledged. Our desire to reach out and experience through using physical senses entered our thought world and created the dream of a physical world. This dream is the Great Mystery. Through this dream, we created forms that could experience a myriad of sensations. The Great Mystery envisioned sight, sound, scent and touch, as well as the gifts of Creativity, Unconditional Love, Universal Wisdom, and Peace. All of the creatures living on every world in the Universe were envisioned in the dream so that the Great Mystery could experience every possible awareness and perception. The dream became reality as the energy from these thoughts began to slow down vibration and gather together to materialize many forms. The First World had begun.

The First World was the world of thoughts manifesting. This was a soft, dreamy world of shimmering thought energy in the process of manifesting form. In the First World, each Spirit Being extended a Vibrational Light Cord from the dream to anchor our creation and to keep us connected to the Vibrational Light Center of the Universe. As we became unique beings, the Vibrational Light Cords became Vibrational Light Centers. Thought energy circulated around these Vibrational Light Centers for many ages, gradually developing into many shapes. As our common awareness solidified in preparation for physical manifestation, we began to separate our thoughts from our source so that we could perceive through individual viewpoints.

In the First World, energy wove threadlike patterns throughout the Universe. Each energy thread would develop into a planet, sun or star, and many Spirit Beings would later come to inhabit these worlds. The energy threads wove around the Vibrational Light Center at the core of the Earth, bringing the seeds of the Great Mystery's dream to fulfill the potential for this world and weaving the Web of Life that connects all creatures. At that time, each Spirit Being that would ever inhabit this planet manifested as a seed inside the Vibrational Light Center of the Earth and dreamed its individual dream for living. As the First World progressed, the energy vibration continued to slow down even more so that our dreams could anchor into form.

The sun fueled the creation of the First World as it shone the bright light of living both day and night, reminding our awakening individual consciousness of the unity of the Great Mystery and the potential of the dream. After a while, the sun retreated so that all of the manifestations of Mother Earth's dream could evolve and take their places.

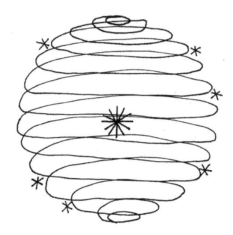

The Second World—Earth Solidifies and Physical Forms Develop

The Second World

In the Second World, the Earth's energy solidified. When the Earth changes occurred, the sun's light was obscured and night descended, bringing with it the reflective light of the moon. The Second World was a dark, womb like place where life developed into its various physical manifestations. Mother Earth's dream manifested the sea to nourish and nurture the creatures to come. Great stone giants rose out of the water to make a place for the creatures to walk. When the Vibrational Light Centers inside Mother Earth felt the vibration shift, we extended our individual Vibrational Light Centers out from the dream and began to nurture physical growth. Each Vibrational Light Center became an individual Spirit Essence. Stones, trees and plants, creature beings, wind, water and fire all took on physical forms. This is when the Spirit Beings entered the Earth Walk, each with individual conscious awareness and a separate ego.

As we stepped into solid physical forms, we developed individual sensations and perceptions. Each Spirit Essence brought gifts and talents to use during our Earth Walk. Since each Spirit Essence manifested a different combination of gifts, our common awareness was now able to experience all the possibilities of the physical world. We were finally ready to experience our dream of learning through sensory perception.

In the Second World, the energy surrounding our planet became a template formed by the thoughts of the Great Mystery's dream. As the planet and all its physical manifestations solidified, an energy thread pulled towards the Earth's Vibrational Light Center and began to spin with a spiraling motion, shaping the Spiral of Life. The Spiral of Life spins in a clockwise direction, from South to North. This most ancient of symbols reflects the process of manifesting the Great Mystery's dream of creation.

In the Second World, individual Spirit Essences separated from the Earth's Vibrational Light Center and began to form separate energy centers. The vibrational frequency of our energy slowed down even more, attracting the physical substances that would be the building blocks of our species. While we moved through the vibrational changes of physical creation, we let go of our awareness of the Great Energy Field and the Universal Mind. Now we could each experience a unique sense of being through many different levels of interaction with all of the other forms of life.

The Ancient Ancestors of each species left the Vibrational Light Center of Mother Earth and swam through the water for many ages before finally climbing out onto land. Each Ancient Ancestor carried special abilities and adaptations that would be encoded in physical form and passed to all of their descendants. All species adapted and evolved as they honed survival skills, perceived through physical senses, and learned the lessons of planetary living. The Second World ended as extreme coldness brought great glaciers that covered the land.

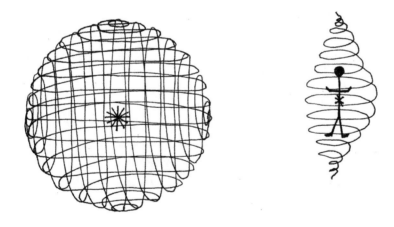

The Third World—Physical Beings Supported by the Spiral of Life

The Third World

The Energy Web around Earth's Vibrational Light Center became unstable during the transition from the Second World into the Third World. The spiral of Earth's Energy Web split and became a double spiral. One spiral continued to flow South to North: The other spiral opposed the first and flowed East to West. The two spirals formed an energy grid surrounding the Earth's Vibrational Light Center but not directly attached to it. This energy flow moved the planet into Third Dimensional existence.

By the Third World, the Earth and all created forms had become solid physical beings existing in the Third Dimension. We were living our dream of perceiving through physical senses and abilities. We maintained our role as creators and continued to manifest our thoughts into innumerable forms and experiences. An environment of wellness and plenty prevailed during the first part of the Third World through the use of technologies that had developed way beyond what we presently know today. We communicated through our thoughts and could perceive in many dimensions. Visitors from the Star Nations interacted with the people as teachers of Universal Wisdom. The Universal Mind was remembered and honored as the Great Mystery, the source of our creation.

In the Third World, humans developed a personal energy flow pattern that mirrored the spiral. Our spiral Energy Webs spun clockwise, starting below our feet and extending beyond our head. Finally, humans carried the Spiral of Life within as each individual Spirit Essence fully developed a physical manifestation. All other forms of life also developed Energy Webs that spiraled. The Energy Webs surrounding each creature, as well as Mother Earth's Energy Web, became solid templates to anchor thoughts into physical reality.

In the Second World, we put too much emphasis on physical creation, and in doing so developed an energy warp where separation began to incubate. As we evolved further into the Third World, the ego became attached to physical possessions, the manifestations of our creation. We spent more time thinking about the forms we created than we did remembering the purpose for our existence—to perceive every possible experience through our individual physical senses. Our consciousness developed a perception of I and sense of separation that began to take priority over our connection to the Great Mystery and the remembrance of unity. By the end of the Third World, we had forgotten that we are all fragments of the same thought awareness and that we shared a common Vibrational Light Center.

Great nations with comfortable ways of living developed in the Third World. The healing arts were highly developed, communication on many levels kept humans in good relationship with the plants, animals and stones, and creativity enabled the manifestation of all our needs. However, as thoughts of separation began to get stronger, their disharmonious vibrations were felt deep in the planetary Vibrational Light Center, once again bringing Earth Changes. The Third World ended with a great flood that split the land, and all living beings, into separate locations.

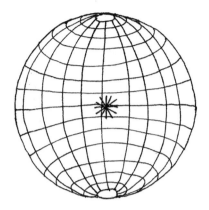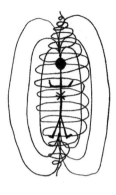

The Fourth World—Separation and Control

The Fourth World

Before the end of the Second World, we lived in a state of blissful awareness. We kept our connection with the Great Mystery and enjoyed the experiences that our creation unfolded. However, as individual egos further developed during the Third World, our perception of individuality created the illusion of separation. Separation fostered greed and brought conflict into being.

During the Fourth World, we created a myriad of separations and evolved as far away as we could go from our common origin. We developed entire systems of thinking and living that separated ourselves from the rest of creation. We saw ourselves as separate entities; not equal to other two-leggeds, the elements, plants, trees, other creature beings, and even Mother Earth. In the end, we separated from our own Spirit Essence, living lonely lives alienated from the very creation that we inspired into being.

As the Fourth World progressed, humans sought to regain our state of blissful awareness. We felt that something was missing when we noticed that the creatures around us lived with blissful awareness and knew that we could also experience this state of being. However, with the exception of a few special people, we never found it because we focused our attention outside ourselves instead of recognizing the dream within our own Spirit Essence. Instead of honoring the many perceptions of our common awareness, we ended up perpetuating a deeper sense of separation.

The energy of the Fourth World separated the double spiral into a square energy grid, intersecting at right angles in the locations where energy centers, or Vortexes, appeared on the surface of the planet. These energy lines were called Ley Lines. Mother Earth's Energy Web no longer resembled the Spiral of Life. In the Fourth World of separation, Mother Earth's Energy Web was not anchored inside her Vibrational Light Center, but was a separate structure surrounding the physical manifestations that we had created.

Humans had evolved into the Fourth Dimension by the time that Earth changes were starting to occur at the end of the Fourth World. Our personal Energy Webs still carried the Spiral of Life, but we had developed a new circular flow of energy that set up a boundary for our Energy Web. This circular energy pathway flowed out of the top of our head, circled around our energy field, and then flowed back in through the soles of our feet, traveling up through our body toward our head. These two energy pathways, the spiral and the circular energy flow, effectively separated our Spirit Essence and physical body from the rest of creation.

Much of the Universal Wisdom available to us in the Third World was limited by our perception of separation as we entered the Fourth World. We were given the opportunity to use our gift of individual will to find our way out of the maze of illusion that we had created. Toward the end of the Fourth World, the Fourth Dimension triggered a reawakening of inner knowing. The energy shifted and some of us remembered the dream. These people began to overcome the limitation of separation and see past the illusion. They began to organize small groups and act collectively. Their actions were noticed and collective groups became common as more and more people began to remember our common roots. As Mother Earth transformed, all people from all lands were feeling the need to change their way of living.

Since 1987, the planet has again been experiencing Earth changes. The dawn of the Fifth World has arrived. Tsunamis, storms, hurricanes, earthquakes, erratic weather patterns and shifting landmasses have rearranged the Fourth World. The institutions of separation that we have created are breaking down through their failure to meet our needs. Politics, economics, religions, education, governments, medicine, languages and national boundaries are all products of the Fourth World that are now collapsing because the energy is no longer here to support these separate ways of thinking and living. Deep within our DNA, we remember the harmony of Mother Earth's heartbeat and the Universal Wisdom. People are now emerging as role models for the Fifth World, creating alternatives to the institutions of separation so that we can once again live in harmony with all of creation and remember who we are.

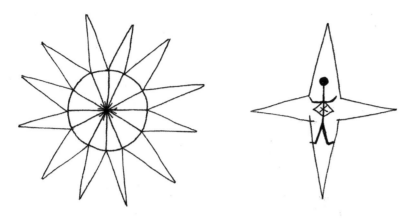

The Fifth World—Remembering Our Creative Purpose

The Fifth World

On August 17, 1987, Mother Earth and all of the creatures that live on this planet entered the transition period from the Fourth World to the Fifth World. This event was popularly known as the Harmonic Convergence, and on that day all Vibrational Light Centers aligned to face the sun. For one moment, we all remembered the Great Mystery and the reason for manifesting the dream of living. A vibration sang out from the Universal Mind within the Great Energy Field and was it was received in the Vibrational Light Center of every Spirit Essence, triggering the memory that we are all connected through the Universal Energy Web—the Web of Life—as one whole, United Being.

Before this time, Mother Earth's Energy Web flowed through the square grids intersecting on and above the planet's surface. Following the Vibrational Alignment in 1987, the old energy grid and Ley Lines dissolved. By October 1990, a new energy formation flowed from within the planet. For the first time in the evolution of the Earth, energy was flowing directly into and out of Mother Earth's Vibrational Light Center at the core of the planet. The results of this energy shift are manifesting now as changes in physical reality on a global, ecological, communal and personal basis.

Our planet's new energy flow looks like a star. Mother Earth's Vibrational Light Center is the center of the star with energy flowing out through the Vortexes on the planet's surface and into the Universe. The Vortexes are located approximately where the energy lines, or Ley Lines, crossed in the Fourth World energy grid. These Vortexes are the places where the planet breathes, or shares energy with the Universe. Now Mother Earth can fully communicate with the Universal Mind.

Likewise, the energy flow around our physical body has changed, taking on the pattern of a star. Our personal Energy Web now flows directly out from our Vibrational Light Center at the core of our being, carrying each person's Vibrational Essence out to greet our Global Family. From our Vibrational Light Center, energy flows down to touch the Vibrational Light Center of Mother Earth, up to touch the Vibrational Light Center of the Great Energy Field, and out in all directions to touch the Energy Webs of all of creatures within the Web of Life. We feel an urgent need to connect our Spirit Essence—our Vibrational Light Center—with the Vibrational Light Centers of all creation as the next step to manifesting the Wholeness of the dream.

As our star energy activates, we remember our purpose through all of the ages of Mother Earth's experience. We recall our common origin and the wisdom that will enable us to reach the flowering of our existence as we rejoin our Vibrational Light Centers back together into One Thought Awareness within the Great Energy Field. The Earth has a dream of creation just as we do. All dreams manifest Wholeness. The unity begins now, as we enter the Fifth World, with some small groups of awakened people coming together to celebrate the Great Mystery and live as One Mind.

When we clear our energy pathways of stress, we become an energy antenna. We open our Energy Web to receive the energy of the Universal Mind and let it flow through our body to nourish and energize Mother Earth. We open our Energy Web to receive the energy from Mother Earth and let it flow through us and out to nourish and energize All Our Relations and the Universe. In this way, we weave wholeness through sharing energy vibrations. The harmony of this energy exchange increases the energy flow around our planet and in the Universe, which in turn increases our vibration and moves us along in evolutionary growth.

Humankind has taken the first step of a major evolutionary development that will rely on bringing the knowledge and perception of our Energy Web into maturity. We presently have the potential to change energy vibrations, to take on the role of Conscious Creators. It is essential that we realize the power of our thoughts to change our Energy Web and manifest corresponding situations. The survival of our species is dependent upon the awakening of our energy body and changing our energy vibration. As chaotic as the Earth Changes may appear at times, they are truly an opportunity to step outside of our limitations and begin this new phase of evolution. We are the ancestors of a new species of humans on this planet.

Earth Changes are proceeding to alter the planet in many ways and each person is adjusting not only to the change in Mother Earth's energy flow, but changes in personal energy flow as well. The year 2012 brought a doorway of evolution where universal energies infused our planet and triggered of a new level of consciousness. This was the beginning of the Fifth World. We are now experiencing more intense vibrational shifts that affect all of creation, moving us beyond physical forms to experience our personal Energy Web. We are gifted with a grand opening of awareness—a new level of energy perception.

Whether we realize it or not, each one of us is learning the Language of Energy and becoming more familiar with our Energy Web. Our physical needs are changing as we accommodate this new energy growth. The rhythm of Mother Earth's heartbeat has changed and we are each adapting to reflect this changed rhythm of life. Issues with health, relationships and living situations are becoming intense as we clear out the old baggage and chose to simplify. We simply can't survive the shift unless we reconcile our differences and accept our unity. Trust that you are experiencing evolution in its most expansive and complete form. As we open our perceptions even wider, we will begin to lose our solid shapes and envision our forms as Energy Beings. The Earth is also changing her physical shape and evolving as an Energy Being. We are making an evolutionary leap, and entering the Fifth Dimension, as we develop into an aware species.

To assist with these Earth Changes and evolutionary developments, the Star People are bringing back the ancient knowledge that we possessed when our awareness was a unified whole. These are not new teachings. We each hold the Wisdom of the Universe within us at all times. Vortex Energy was common knowledge in the first three worlds and was taught in special places of learning. As we entered the Fourth World, this knowledge was obscured from our memories so that we could learn the lessons of separation. Now as we enter the Fifth World, the wisdom of the Vortex is being returned to humankind so that we can remember our common energy body and reunite with the Universal Vibrational Light Center that is the Great Mystery.

The Sixth World—Spirit Essences Sharing One Energy Web

The Sixth World

In the Fifth World, we will achieve the awareness of Wholeness; first in the physical dimension by recognizing and honoring our common origins, and then in the energy dimension by connecting the energy of our Vibrational Light Centers together. When we evolve into the Sixth World, humans and the Earth will share the same energy flow pattern and the same Energy Web.

In the Sixth World, we will reach the goal of our creation. Now, we will finally be able to experience physical living through individual perception as a common awareness. When our goal is realized, we will no longer need physical forms, such as our bodies. The Earth, all of the plants, stones, trees, creatures and humans will take on the form of our Spirit Essences and become Energy Beings. Although we will retain individual energy forms, we will perceive awareness as many sensors of the same mind. Language will no longer be necessary, as all perception will be experienced and received by everyone simultaneously. We will expand into the Sixth, Seventh, Eighth and Ninth Dimensions and beyond.

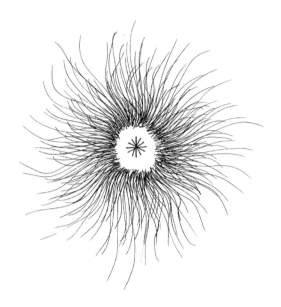

The Seventh World—Becoming Unity—the Dream Realized

The Seventh World

In the Seventh World, all of creation will join together to complete the Great Mystery's Dream. We will merge back into the Vibrational Light Center of the Universal Mind within the Great Energy Field, returning to the unity where we originated. The Earth will become embodied within the unity of our merging, and our energy will shine together brighter than ever before. When we step beyond our energy forms, we will become Light Beings and the Earth will become a new star. Beyond the light is the sound of a common voice. Our creation complete, we will be reborn as a single Spirit Being—one Vibrational Light Essence—with the experience and expansive knowledge of physical form. We will emerge from our cocoon as an entirely new thought creation.

PART TWO: YOUR PERSONAL ENERGY WEB

Are you one of the Shining Ones?

Do you feel an intense purpose and commitment for your life?
Can you feel changes that are going to occur before they happen?
Do you feel connected to the environment with the very core of your being?
Do you have strong feelings and impressions that are difficult to put into words?
Can you communicate with plants and animals or tell what other people are thinking?
Do you look out at the stars and wonder where we came from in this vast Universe?
Are you aware of the vibrational essence of life all around you?

If you experience any of these characteristics on a regular basis, then you may be one of the Shining Ones. The Shining Ones are part of the Matrix of the Universal Energy Web that manifests the Dream of Living. The Shining Ones resonate with a quicker, more expanded vibrational frequency than other people, which makes them sensitive to energy, so sensitive that they react to the energy around them and may even appear to take on energy. The Shining Ones instinctively know how to communicate through energy exchange. They can feel the spark of life in a plant, a tree, or a stone. They know the intention in the walk of an animal or the look in someone's eye. The crystal light energy within the Shining Ones enables them to perceive in many dimensions. They sympathetically feel the experience of others, making them especially talented in maintaining close contact with friends and loved ones even when they are separated by distance. This same ability makes the Shining Ones exceptional healers, as they know exactly what is needed. The Web of Life, the invisible Energy Web that connects all life in the Universe, is easily perceived by the Shining Ones.

The Shining Ones can sense a change of vibration and know a little bit about what that change will be. For example, a Shining One may think of someone and that person will call or appear very shortly. A Shining One may also intuitively know when personal changes are on the horizon way before the signs appear, and they will prepare by focusing their thoughts on manifesting new opportunities. Many Shining Ones can foretell a change in the weather or know when a major shift is happening somewhere on the planet, even as far away as the other side of the Earth. Much like the ripples that go out to cover the entire pond when a stone is thrown in, the Shining Ones feel the intensity of vibration that ripples out from the Earth Changes.

The Shining Ones are fully aware of life around them because their emotional awareness and physical body can perceive the subtle energy vibrations that exist in many dimensions. Because they respond to minute energy fluctuations, the Shining Ones can appear moody, hyperactive, or overly sensitive. In reality, the Shining Ones are mirroring the emotional or environmental climate in a given area or situation through these emotional states. The Shining Ones perceive a deep level of connection with all living things and the environment. Learning how to balance this energy will help us learn how to balance our relationships, physical health, emotional outlook and even the Earth's environment.

The physical body of a Shining One resonates with the same vibration as a quartz crystal. Like the quartz crystal, the energy of a Shining One attracts others through the rainbows that it gives off. The Shining Ones can be energy generators, giving off energy that others can use, usually as inspiration and motivation. They can also be healers, rejuvenating others simply by touching their energy. When the Shining Ones are in close proximity with others, the energy connection they make opens up pathways within the Universal Energy Web. The Shining Ones must be nurtured to keep their energy vibration attuned; therefore it is important for the Shining Ones to replenish their energy frequently. A clear quartz crystal is the best emotional stabilizer and physical and emotional rejuvenator for the Shining Ones. Drinking water in which a clear quartz crystal has been placed in sunlight or moonlight for several hours is a most nourishing elixir for the Shining One's body, mind and spirit.

If you have picked up this book, you are consciously evolving with the Earth changes. By now, you probably recognize the consciousness of the Shining Ones within yourself or others. The Shining Ones are manifesting on the Earth at this time to assist with the evolution of our planet. The rules that applied in the past do not necessarily support the increased vibration and awareness that the Shining Ones have to offer. The Shining Ones need to be allowed the timing and space in which they can most comfortably function. This may mean rearranging schedules to allow for integration time, a space to balance energy before heading out to another activity. It may require avoiding places with strong electromagnetic energy—such as shopping malls—and limiting exposure to large crowds.

Because the Shining Ones are influenced by the energy of everything they come into contact with, they often develop allergies to things with dissimilar vibrations. It is very important for Shining Ones to eat consciously, with awareness of various types of food, and choose the best food for nourishment on all levels—physically, emotionally and energetically. Food and healing methods should be intuitively selected through listening to what the body needs. Clean water is a vital element for Shining Ones and should be included every day for both drinking and bathing. Care should be taken with clothes, cleaning products, and all things that the Shining Ones come into contact with.

The Shining Ones need to sit on the Earth frequently—ideally every day—so they can reconnect with the heartbeat of Mother Earth, the rhythm generated by the Vibrational Light Center of the planet. The Shining Ones need extra quiet time for staying balanced so that their sensitive energy does not get stretched beyond their limits or drained. Often, the Shining Ones are loners. They are so different from their peers that they do not fit in with the group. Time alone allows the Shining Ones to nourish their Spirit Essence and maintain important energy connections with the Universe and the Earth. It is also important for the Shining Ones to explore creativity, as energy vibrations are more easily expressed through color, line, form, movement and sound than words. Goals that seem important in the material world are of little concern to a Shining One, who is more interested in creating, experiencing and being in nature than in money and systems that require conforming to specific ideals.

The Shining Ones manifest Vortex Energy in physical form. They instinctively know how to focus, direct and rearrange energy. They are drawn to natural energy centers and the places on the Earth that need healing. People are drawn by the Shining Ones' magnetic energy and charisma.

But the Shining Ones are not manifesting only in human form. Certain trees, plants, animals, and even the Spirits of water, wind and fire are Shining Ones. You will know when you find a Shining One by the energy that they have to share, for the Shining Ones radiate rainbows in their Energy Webs.

The Shining Ones are living at this time to: Inspire humans to focus their thoughts to create a future based on peace and harmony; Help us remember the Web of Life that connects all creatures; Awaken our commitment to act responsibly; and Trigger the awakening of all 12 strands of our DNA so that humans can evolve with the planet to become one living being. We are all evolving. Each of us will eventually adapt the consciousness of the Shining Ones as our DNA awakens and our energy vibration increases.

At this time in our evolution, we are jumping the gap between dimensions, fulfilling the prophecies of the Ancient Wisdom Keepers of all Nations. The Shining Ones have manifested now in physical bodies to awaken the genetic coding that is necessary for the survival of the planet. We are the ancestors of the new species of humans who will create a world of peace and harmony, fully realizing our gift of creative manifestation—creating reality through focused thoughts.

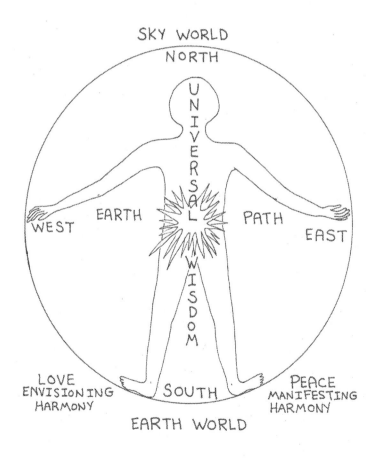

Our Medicine Wheel Connection

Our Energy Web and the Medicine Wheel

We can use the Medicine Wheel and its traditional teachings as a foundation for interpreting Vortex energy. Medicine is Spirit connection, Wheel is Energy for growth; thus the Medicine Wheel is the Energy that directs our Spirit Essence through the Earth Walk. The Medicine Wheel includes the teachings of the Four Directions, our connection to Mother Earth and father Sky, and ceremonies and dances that help us to remember the Great Mystery and our purpose for being. The center of the Medicine Wheel is an Energy Vortex that connects us with the Web of Life. The Universal Wisdom Pathway opens our awareness to Universal Wisdom and grounds us with an Earth Connection. The Earth Path provides the opportunities to seek our vision and share our gifts with others. These two pathways cross at the center of the Medicine Wheel, our Vibrational Light Center, where all that we are manifests as the Truth of our being. The Truth encoded within your personal Medicine Wheel includes your purpose for living, your understanding of Universal Wisdom, a connection with your Guardian Spirit and Medicine Plant, and the colors, sounds, and abilities that make you who you are. All life follows the Medicine Wheel, moves in cycles, and manifests its own individual Truth.

The Medicine Wheel cycle is symbolized by the Four Directions that sit on the circle plus three directions that connect us to Mother Earth, Father Sky and our Spirit Essence. We begin our Earth Walk in the Direction of the South, the place of New Beginnings. In the South, we recognize our connection with all other life—the four-leggeds, winged ones, water creatures, other two-leggeds, even stone people, plant people and tree people. We are all connected by blood (chlorophyll is chemically similar to blood), thus we are All Relations, all Children of Mother Earth. We walk through the South with innocence and open-mindedness, receptive to all possibilities and potential. There are no preconceived thoughts as we look around and get to know All Our Relations and this planet that is our home. Like children, we unconditionally accept the gifts of all that we come into contact with. When our feet touch the ground for the first time, we feel Mother Earth's heartbeat and carry it within us throughout our entire time here. We always maintain our connection with Mother Earth, and through that Earth Connection we know that we are never alone.

The Direction of the West is the place of Inner Knowing. We experience the West through silence, the place where we go within to hear our inner wisdom and guidance. Here we can look with our inner Spirit Eyes, listen with our inner Spirit Ears, and feel with the energy strands that extend from our heart. In the West, we communicate with our Guardian Spirit, Plant Teachers and Ancestors. We enter the Dreamtime and receive intuitive messages. There is no need to fear the absolute darkness of the West, for our Guardian Spirit is always ready to guide us. In the Direction of the West, we can envision the future and dream our own dream for living. Within the darkness of the West, we can find strength and focus through knowing our Spirit Essence.

The North is the direction of Wisdom and Gratitude. The Trickster Spirit sits here, bringing lessons that challenge us to become the very best that we can be. Sometimes we must receive the most difficult lessons in order to find healing and wisdom, but healing and wisdom are always there behind the challenges and pain. We recognize that healing comes only when we are grateful for our lessons. When begin each day with gratitude, we find the beauty in all things. In the Direction of the North, we honor the Teachers and Elders who share their experiences so that we may grow. We recognize our own inner wisdom and know that the answers to all of our questions can be found within. The wisdom of the North calls us to utilize the messages of the West through making wise choices based on creating healing and peaceful relationships.

The Direction of the East is the place of Inspiration and Creativity. In the East, we know that our potential is unlimited; for within the Great Mystery's dream exists everything we need. There is more than enough for all creatures. In the East, we recognize that our thoughts are like seeds that will grow into reality. When we accept changes in our life, we bring new ideas onto the Earth Walk to create the situations that we visualized. The East brings the gift of creative expression and calls us to explore communication on many levels. To live in a harmonious way, we are inspired to keep good feelings, good thoughts, good words and good actions; for we know that all of these will eventually go out on the Web of Life to touch All Our Relations.

The Direction above our head on the Medicine Wheel is the Sky World. The Sky World surrounds and protects Mother Earth. From this direction, we receive the gifts of Father Sky and the Wisdom of the Universe. We honor the Sky World by simply taking a deep breath and breathing in the energy of life. We look to the sky, observe the life-giving light of Grandfather Sun and learn the gift of being unconditional; for the sun's light is available to all without qualifications. In the Direction of the Sky World, we can connect with the Universal Mind and have access to the knowledge upon which the Universal Laws are structured. We recognize that our Earth Family has many Relations in this vast Universe and that the entire Universe functions with a rhythm that includes, but is more expanded than, the Earth's cycles and our own personal rhythms. The Sky World is the direction where we access information from the Star People who are our teachers.

The Direction below our feet on the Medicine Wheel is the Earth World. In this direction, we make the connection to Mother Earth that is the foundation for our Earth Walk. We recognize ourselves as Spirit (energy) Beings in earth bodies that came here specifically to connect with the knowledge and experience of the Earth. Mother Earth gives us all that we need for living and takes care of All Our Relations as well. As Spirit Beings, we have a responsibility to give back to Mother Earth so that each step we take is based on Universal Wisdom, shares Unconditional Love, and creates Peace. In the Direction of the Earth World, we remember the purpose for our Earth Walk and the commitment we made when we were born. We know that upon whatever path we chose, our feet always touch the Earth, so our energy is rooted in the Earth like the trees. We also recognize that Mother Earth is a living being with a purpose and a dream that is greater than the dreams of any of the creatures that live on her surface. Mother Earth has always existed, she manifests the many forms of life around us now, and she will continue to exist and transform within the Rhythm of the Universe. The story of Earth is the story of beauty manifesting; the wisdom of Earth is survival.

The Seventh Direction is inside each of us. The center of the Medicine Wheel is our Vibrational Light Center where our Spirit Essence resides and where we maintain our connection to the Great Mystery. When we first envisioned this Earth Walk, we sent an energy thread, a Vibrational Light Cord, out to anchor our Vibrational Light Center in a physical body. Our Vibrational Light Center became the center of our personal Medicine Wheel, the location where universal energy enters our physical body through our Energy Web, and where we connect with all Our Relations in the Web of Life.

We are centered when our awareness is fully present in the center of our personal Medicine Wheel. We perceive with the open-mindedness of the South; we access the gifts of the West to listen and look within; we experience the wisdom and healing of the North; and we are inspired to create in the East. When we are centered, we honor the Universal Wisdom that comes from the Sky World Above; we feel the foundation of the Earth World Below our feet; and we know who we are and why we are here based on the personal Truth that we carry within our Vibrational Light Center. This is the place where we must stand in order to use the Vortex. The Vortex is not intended to be used with a condition or specific vision of healing or change. Rather, through the Vortex we open to Universal Wisdom and let energy rearrange according to the greater plan of the Great Mystery's dream. Before beginning Vortex work on yourself or others, always take a few moments to clear out your energy and return your awareness to your Vibrational Light Center. If you are unable to do this, then it is not the right time for Vortex work, try again later.

Once you are centered, visualize yourself standing in the center of the Medicine Wheel. (See Illustration) Your feet are standing in the foundation of the South and your head is in the wisdom of the North. You are walking in trust with an open mind while honoring your inner wisdom and guidance. From the bottom of your feet to the top of your head (South to North) is your Universal Wisdom Pathway, the main energy pathway that connects you to both the Earth and Universe, and it corresponds to the same path on the Medicine Wheel.

Your left hand is where you receive inspiration through Spirit messages and guidance. Your right hand is where your achievements are manifested through creative thought (West to East). This is your Earth Path, the main energy pathway that connects us to others, and it corresponds to the same path on the Medicine Wheel. If you draw both of your hands into the center of your body, placing the right hand over the left hand, you cover your Vibrational Light Center. This is where you connect with the Great Mystery and the Web of Life.

Now visualize your Energy Web extending outward from your Heart Center and Vibrational Light Center. Your Energy Web is the energy body that surrounds your physical body like the circle that surrounds the Medicine Wheel. Thoughts, feelings, emotions and dreams are carried within your Energy Web. Notice how your energy flows in a circular path surrounding your Sacred Space. As our energy flows, we can choose to extend energy lines out to connect with others or simply allow the energy to continue spiraling to renew and replenish our body, mind and spirit. As our energy spirals it sparkles, reflecting the Spirit Essence we carry within. You can see the sparkle of someone's Spirit Essence when you look deeply into their eyes.

Now you are prepared to use the Vortex. Breathe deeply and take a few moments to experience the energy of your personal Medicine Wheel.

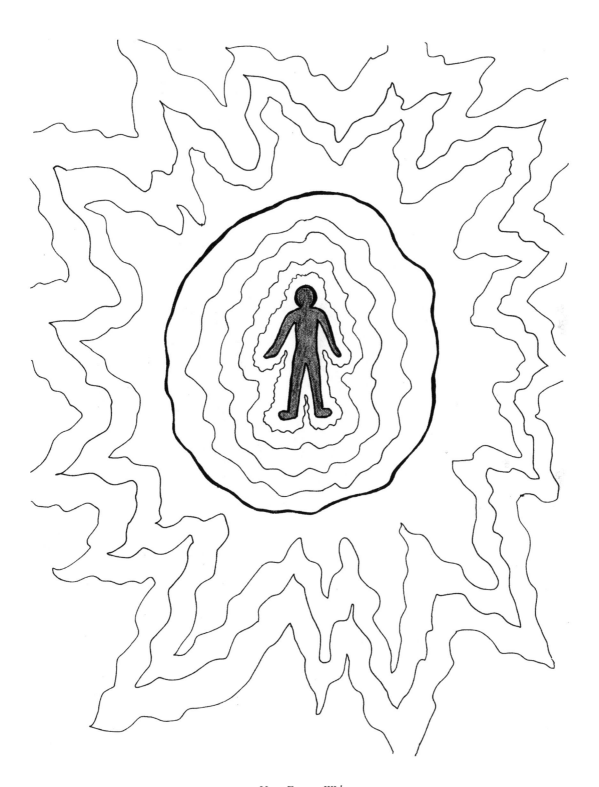

Your Energy Web

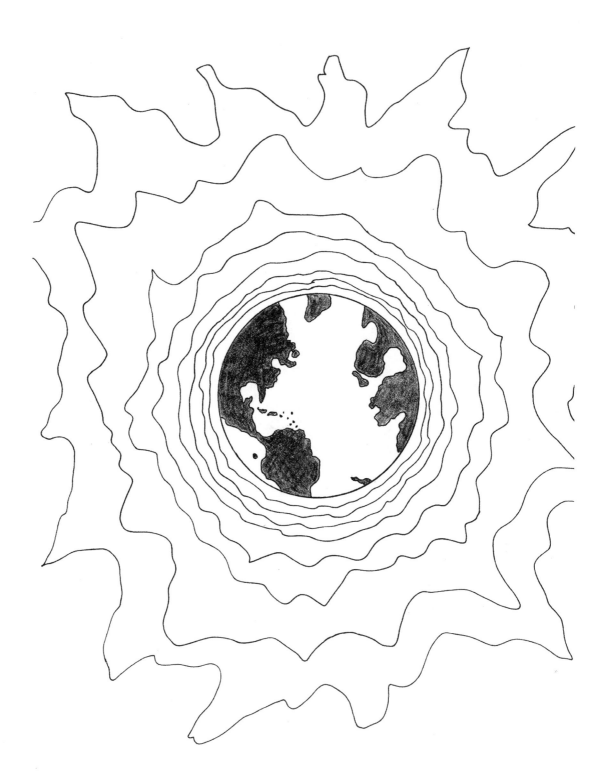

Mother Earth's Energy Web

Our Energy Web, Vortex Energy Centers and Energy Lines

We already know that the Universe is comprised of millions of Energy Webs and that many of these Energy Webs interact with our personal Energy Web to influence our perception and experience of living. Our Energy Web carries vibrational sensors that cue us in to the energy in the environment and other creatures.

Your personal Energy Web carries the blueprint for who you are and why you are here. It surrounds your physical body and contains all of your feelings, thoughts, emotions and dreams. The first contact that you make with others is through your Energy Web.

Your personal Energy Web is a series of concentric circles, anchored within your Vibrational Light Center and extending out to form the boundary of your Sacred Space. Your boundary separates you from the rest of the Web of Life and is your initial contact with the outside world. You can strengthen your boundary to protect your Sacred Space, or you can extend your Fine Lines out past your boundary to connect with the Energy Webs of other creature beings that you come into contact with. Your personal vibration is continually communicated through your Energy Web. On an unconscious level, we are exchanging energy all of the time. This means that opportunities are there for us to take on the emotional projections of others, or for us to dump our emotional baggage onto them, all without conscious intention or thought.

The energy circles between your physical body and the boundary of your Energy Web are where thoughts and emotions reside. Our thoughts travel outward, gather energy from their corresponding emotions, and then proceed through our Fine Lines to connect with similar vibrations in the Universe that will manifest their physical forms. This is why we can either consciously or inadvertently affect others through energy exchange.

We can set up a comfort monitor to filter unacceptable thoughts and energy from entering through our boundary. This brings the energy exchange into our conscious awareness where we can choose to accept or release any energy. Once we have accepted an outside energy, it travels inward, bringing its corresponding emotion into our Sacred Space. If we decide to keep the emotion, it travels through our Energy Web and eventually affects our physical being with healing or disease depending upon the emotion involved. All energy is neutral until we decide to accept it into our personal Energy Web. Our personal philosophy of living, and the way we react to the emotion connected to the energy, determines the effect that it will have on us.

Our personal Energy Web anchors the universal energy flow within our physical form. We create a physical and emotional body corresponding to our expectations within the energy circles where our emotions reside. This is where our Energy Web is most fluid and flexible. Each thought that we have is an Energy Construct that programs our Energy Web. It is easy to change the programming, providing both the thought and corresponding emotions are brought into balance and focused with clear intention upon the new construct. Health, well being, physical appearance, and the situations that we experience in our life are all constructs that we have created within our Energy Web.

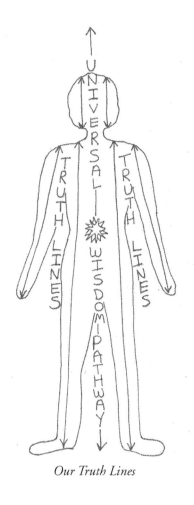

Our Truth Lines

Truth Lines

Our Energy Web is made up of energy lines that are the pathways along which energy flows, and energy centers that are the locations where energy enters and exits our Energy Web.

The Universal Wisdom Pathway anchors Universal and Earth energies within your Vibrational Light Center. Since these energies become your Truth, we will call all the energy lines that run from your head down through your feet Truth Lines. The Universal Wisdom Pathway runs from above your head, down through your spinal column, along the long bones of your arms and legs, through the bones of your hands and feet, and then extends out into the Earth through the Energy Centers below your feet. After connecting with the Earth, the Universal Wisdom Pathway flows out to the boundary of your Sacred Space, circles up to reach the universal energy above your head, and back down to flow through your body. The Universal Wisdom Pathway is one of your Truth Lines, and there are many other Truth Lines that run through your body parallel to the Universal Wisdom Pathway. Your Truth Lines form the concentric circles of your Energy Web and anchor your Truth—your purpose and commitment for this Earth Walk.

When we are anchored in our Truth, we are doing what we came here to do, and energy flows freely along our Truth Lines. Our pathways of connection to both the Universal Mind and the Sacred Cave of Mother Earth are open so that we can channel energy through us from Mother Earth and Father Sky as we walk. When we are anchored in our Truth, our energy is centered within us. Energy is not pulled out in front of us with future concerns, or trailing behind us with unresolved past experiences that might hold us back. Neither is energy pulled out to either side of us, focused on the responsibility of others. We are centered within our personal Sacred Space, our thoughts are based on Unconditional Love, and our actions are focused on creating Peace. When energy flows freely along our Truth Lines, we fulfill our part of the Universal Dream and our own purpose for living.

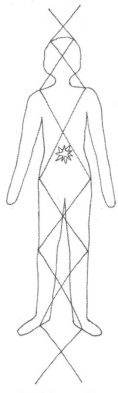

Our Memory Lines

Memory Lines

Encoded within our Memory Lines is our purpose for this Earth Walk and our memories of the past. Our Memory Lines look like four x's connected together, each one sitting directly on top of the one underneath it, with the center of the x's crossing on the Universal Wisdom Pathway. The first x goes from either side of the top of the head to the shoulders, crossing within our Sensory Centers. The second x goes from right shoulder to left hip and left shoulder to right hip, crossing at our Vibrational Light Center. The next x is from the right hip to the left knee and the left hip to the right knee. The final x goes from the right knee to the bottom of the left foot and the left knee to the bottom of the right foot. The x's that make up our Memory Lines continue out from the top of the head into the Universe, and from the bottom of our feet into the Earth.

Because our Memory Lines flow from both sides of the body through our Universal Wisdom Pathway, energy flowing through them maintains physical balance. Usually, the rhythm of the right and left sides of our body is different. The left side is the nourishing side of our body, where we bring in energy and inspiration. The right side is the giving side of our body, where we extend energy out to others. When we bring the energy of both sides of our body together, like when we put the palms of our hands together, we allow the rhythms of our right and left sides to blend together. This circle completes within our Vibrational Light Center, resulting with a harmonious overall energy from the blending of these two rhythms.

Energy flowing along our Memory Lines triggers our DNA. The individual thread of Grandmother Spider's Web that we carry manifests its form as our DNA. Encoded within our DNA is the Great Mystery's dream, our purpose for living, our gifts and talents for this Earth Walk, and all of the memories of our physical ancestors. Vibrations, geometric shapes, colors and sounds arrange the coding of our DNA and awaken the energy flow along our Memory Lines. When energy flows unobstructed along our Memory Lines, we have the ability to change the blueprint of who we are by accessing and reprogramming our DNA. As the Earth changes progress, vibrations within the rhythm of life are changing, and this will manifest through our DNA as physical adaptations to enable survival. When you chant your personal vibration, your Memory Lines will clear and enable your DNA to shift into the pattern best suited for your evolution. When this happens, you will begin to remember the past all the way back to the origin of the Dream of Living. As the vibration of wholeness becomes strong, energy flowing along our Memory Lines will bring increased balance and well being into our life.

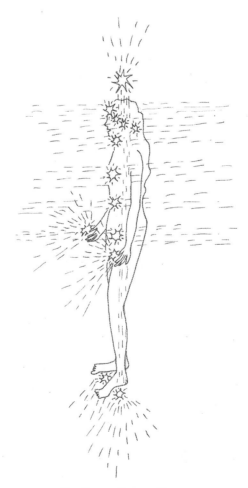

Our Vortex Energy Centers

Vortex Energy Centers

We have Energy Centers, or Energy Vortexes, that are located at the places in our body where energy is exchanged between our Energy Web and our physical form. Each Vortex Energy Center is like a tube spanning every layer of our concentric energy circles, and then connecting with one of the organs that govern our primary body functions. Energy flows through these centers horizontally, front to back. As upright creatures, we are constantly moving through the concentric energy circles that extend out into the atmosphere from the matrix of Mother Earth's Energy Web. When our Vortex Energy Centers are open, the energy from Mother Earth's concentric circles flows through us as we walk.

We can work with the Vortex Energy Centers at every layer of our Energy Web and within many layers inside our physical body. For the purpose of the exercises in this book, we will work with the Vortex Energy Centers located at the point where the Energy Web and physical body meet.

The first Vortex Energy Center, our Center of Universal Awareness, sits in the Energy Web above our head and connects us with Universal Wisdom. The Center of Universal Awareness filters everything that comes into our presence so that we can experience it within our perspective of Truth. The Fine Lines that extend from the Center of Universal Awareness connect us with the Universal Mind.

The Thought Center, our second Vortex Energy Center, sits inside of our brain. Our thoughts originate in our Thought Center. This is the place of conscious awareness, where we interpret sensory experiences and develop psychic awareness. The Thought Center enables us to connect with others through many dimensions of nonverbal communication. Here is where we envision what we wish to manifest. When we think positive thoughts, we create harmony in our life.

Our third Vortex Energy Center is comprised of the two Sensory Centers that bring input into our Thought Center. These include the eye, ear, nose, and mouth on the right side of the head and the same sensory organs on the left side. Since the rhythms of both sides of the body are different, the organs in each Sensory Center work together to create an image from their combined perspectives that is then sent to the Thought Center for evaluation. Energy traveling through these centers can allow us to see beyond the depth of our physical vision and hear beyond the scope of our physical ears.

Our fourth Vortex Energy Center, the Throat Center, is our Communication Center. This is where our words originate. We are able to share sounds and words with others through our Communication Center, giving us the ability to respond to information gathered by our sensory center. The Fine Lines extending from our Throat Center help us give form to our visions. When we speak positive words, we share harmony with others.

Our fifth Vortex Energy Center is our Heart Center. Thoughts and actions are balanced in the Heart Center, where our Earth Path manifests in our physical body. Our Heart Center is the Center of Doing. This is where our feelings originate. The Fine Lines that flow out from the heart establish relationships with others and attract the situations that we feel ready to accept. The Fine Line connections of the Heart Center influence our thoughts and actions more than the

Fine Lines of any other Vortex Energy Center. When we share positive feelings with others, we create harmonious relationships.

Connected to the Heart Center through the pathways of our Truth Lines and Memory Lines are two Creative Centers, one in each hand. The two Creative Centers comprise our sixth Vortex Energy Center. Creative inspirations are received through our left hand and creative ideas are manifested through our right hand. This is the pathway of energy through the Heart Center. It does not imply that people should be right-handed or left-handed. When energy flows freely through the Heart Center, our emotions and inspirations can be expressed through either or both hands. When our Heart Center is clear, we are in a place of giving and receiving Unconditional Love. Our gift of creativity is unrestricted and can manifest freely, creating many expressions of the beauty around us.

Our seventh Vortex Energy Center, our physical Center of Being, is located just above the navel. The Center of Being is our most Sacred Space because through it we connect with the Web of Life and the Great Mystery. This is the place where our Spirit Essence resides in our physical body. Our Vibrational Light Center is connected within our Center of Being, so we can also refer to this center as our Vibrational Light Center. Here is where our actions originate. Most of our Fine Lines originate in our Vibrational Light Center. From the Vibrational Light Center, energy moves out through all of our energy pathways to nourish our physical body and Energy Web. The amount of energy that we feel at any given time is directly related to the energy flowing through our Vibrational Light Center. When energy is flowing freely through our Vibrational Light Center, we have the motivation and enthusiasm to actively participate in living. When energy is blocked in our Vibrational Light Center, we may constantly feel tired or develop systemic imbalances that reflect the lack of life energy flowing through our body. When we share positive actions, we manifest harmony in the world.

Our eighth Vortex Energy Center, our Reproductive Center, grounds our self-image with our Earth Connection. This is the place where our sexual connections originate. This Energy Center is located within our sexual organs. The Reproductive Center manifests our gender choice and determines how we use our gifts and learn our lessons in this Earth Walk. For females, this gift is nourishing, for males this gift is protecting. Of course, every person has both male and female aspects within their being. We experience inner balance whenever energy is flowing freely through our Reproductive Center. Our sexual energy is then ready to be shared with another person. Through this union, we connect the Spirit World with the Earth Walk to manifest reality.

Extending from our Reproductive Center are two Grounding Centers located on the bottom of each foot. They comprise our ninth Vortex Energy Center. The Grounding Centers connect to our Reproductive Center through the pathways of our Truth Lines and Memory Lines. Through our Grounding Centers, we connect Mother Earth's heartbeat with our own heartbeat to create a circle of energy that strengthens our Earth Connection. We receive the vibration of the Earth through our left foot; it travels to our Vibrational Light Center to merge with our personal vibration, and is returned to the Earth through our right foot. When energy travels freely through our Reproductive Center, we feel grounded and satisfied with ourselves. Fertility is within the control of our thoughts and we can choose when or when not to create new life. We then experience an inner balance of nurturing and protecting that brings a wholeness of being.

There are many other small Vortex Energy Centers throughout our body and each one plays an important role for attuning the energy vibrations traveling along our energy pathways. Many of the Vortex Energy Centers are located at our joints. In our hands and feet, where there is a concentration of Vortex Energy Centers, we can create geometric energy configurations that weave energy patterns through our actions. These are the skills that you will learn in this workbook. There are Vortex Energy Centers located within the brain that enable perception, and Vortex Energy centers within the DNA that enable manifestation. We can work with any or all of our Vortex Energy Centers.

When energy flows freely through all of our Vortex Energy Centers, we feel a deep calmness that is relaxing and healing. Our body functions smoothly within its own natural rhythm, and we experience a physical and emotional balance that establishes well being. Mother Earth's concentric energy circles flow through us, and we embody the Oneness of the Web of Life.

Our Fine Lines

Fine Lines

Our Fine Lines are the energy strands that connect our Spirit Essence to our Energy Web, consciousness, and physical body. The Fine Lines are the part of our Energy Web that can extend past the boundary of our Sacred Space to establish an energy connection with the outside world. Most of our Fine Lines originate inside of our Center of Being (within our Vibrational Light Center) and travel outwards to connect with other creatures and places in the Universe, but Fine Lines can also originate in other Vortex Energy Centers, most commonly our Heart Center and Thought Center. We connect with the Web of Life, Mother Earth and the Universe through our Fine Lines. We also connect to the Great Mystery and bring the life giving energy of Father Sky into our body through our Fine Lines.

Energy continually flows into our Fine Lines from the sun, the moon, and other planets and stars in our Universal Family. These heavenly bodies give off a vibration encoded with light, color, sound, electromagnetic energy, and geometric shapes that travels through our Fine Lines to connect with our personal vibration inside of our Vibrational Light Center. The coming together of these vibrations triggers our memory of Universal Wisdom and Universal Law. When we send out a thought for manifestation, it travels through all of the concentric circles of our Energy Web, then out through our Fine Lines to attract similar energy from the Void. Our Fine Lines connect us to the Void at all times so that every thought we have has the potential to affect what we create in our life.

When we meet others, the first thing we do is to connect energy through touching our Fine Lines. The magnetism created by the interactions of two different vibrational fields gives us an initial feeling of comfort or uneasiness with the other person. If we are perceptive to the Universal Language of Energy, we can assess the other person's Fine Lines. When we establish a close, caring relationship, a connection is made between the Fine Lines of both people. This enables us to sense how the other person is feeling without verbal or physical communication. After that, energy is always shared between the two, no matter how far apart we are. When we bond with another person, one of their Fine Lines attaches to our Heart Center and one of our Fine Lines attaches to theirs. The connection between mother and child is a particularly strong Fine Line bond that originates inside the womb. Sexual relationships also create strong energy bonds, for through this special connection, we anchor one of our partner's Fine Lines within our Reproductive Center and one of our Fine Lines within theirs.

The flow of energy through our Fine Lines directly affects our awareness of the Universe and the world around us. Our Spirit Essence is nourished by the energy vibrations that flow through our Fine Lines. We internalize the life giving energy of Father Sky and experience inner harmony through our Fine Lines. If the energy flowing through our Fine Lines becomes inhibited, our life force weakens.

The Earth Walk is but one reality in a series of dimensions that fit together like slightly overlapping concentric circles. Some of these dimensions, like color, sound and rhythm, can be experienced while we live in a physical body here on Earth. Other dimensions exist closer to the Spirit World and can be visited only while we are in the Dreamtime. There are also dimensions where the vibrational frequency is too different for our mental and physical abilities to comprehend through our physical senses at this time. When we develop our ability to perceive energy, we can experience some of these other dimensions through our Fine Lines. When our Spirit Essence returns to the Great Mystery at the completion of our Earth Walk, we will experience all of the dimensions of reality simultaneously. In the Fifth World, as we become balanced physical and spiritual beings, we will learn to use our Fine Lines to perceive many more dimensions of the Universe around us.

Our Truth Lines, Memory Lines, Vortex Energy Centers, and Fine Lines make up our personal Energy Web. All other people, creatures, stones, trees and plants have similar energy pathways and Vortex Energy Centers within their personal Energy Webs. The Energy Webs of all of Mother Earth's Children are concentric circles anchored within their Vibrational Light Centers and enclosed by the boundary of their Sacred Space. The Energy Web of each creature being carries their commitment for living and creates the pattern for their physical form of existence. Within each creature being's Vibrational Light Center is their connection to Great Mystery's light and from here, Fine Lines extend out to connect with other creatures and places on the Earth and in the Universe. The vibrational sensors in our Fine Lines can cue us in to the energy in the environment or even energy from events that occurred in a specific location during different time periods. As all living beings walk through Mother Earth's Energy Web, their Fine Lines channel energy from Mother Earth to the Universe and back. When energy is flowing freely through the individual Energy Webs of all the creature beings, the Web of Life vibrates with the rhythm of the dance of life unfolding.

The Open Vortex Doorway

First Light of a new vibration,

A very small change

Unnoticed by those who do not closely observe,

Creeps in and surrounds us like a warm, cozy blanket.

Nestled securely, we innocently dream

Not knowing that we are envisioning our future.

We let our wings unfold

And allow magic to happen,

Astonished by its beauty and simplicity.

This brings peace into our hearts

And love into our actions.

Awakening happens on many levels.

The dream, enmeshed within our Energy Web

Walks with us as possibility.

The Vortex opens.

Energy Vibration embraces possibility.

Things will never be the same.

PART THREE: THE VORTEX

The Vortex is the doorway to the Universal Mind. When we put things in the Vortex, the resonance of their vibration changes, rearranging the Energy Web and physical manifestation to function in harmony with the Universal Rhythm.

Each creature is born with the ability of Unconditional Love along with the unlimited potential that is possible when that love is shared. Love (or lack of love) creates our thought-reality; for in order to manifest our vision, it must be aligned with the vibration of Unconditional Love. Unconditional Love is our motivation for creating good thoughts, speaking good words, honoring good feelings and sharing through good relationships to create Peace. When all of our thoughts and actions are based on Unconditional Love, that love multiplies and returns to nourish our own life. We each bring a piece of Universal Wisdom to the Earth Walk and this is our personal Truth. For us to live in balance, we must always express our Universal Wisdom. Peace is the basis for all of our actions. We must always consider the consequences of our actions for the next seven generations to come and we must never impose our personal beliefs on the process of another creature's growth. When we use our gifts of Unconditional Love, Truth based on Universal Wisdom and Peace, when we listen to our Spirit Essence, and when we honor our connection to the Great Mystery and the Web of Life, then we are centered— living in harmony.

Your body exists within the electromagnetic field of your Energy Web. Your Energy Web continually manifests and programs your physical body while energizing and protecting your Sacred Space. Traveling out from your Vortex Energy Centers, electromagnetic energy pathways take life-giving energy to all parts of your physical and energetic body.

Everyday we encounter many ways in which this energy flow gets out of balance. Extreme or prolonged stress pulls us away from our center and drains our energy. Physical trauma, illness or injury changes our energy flow pattern. Environmental factors, such as exposure to natural disasters and weather conditions, affect the electromagnetic charge of our energy (The most dramatic is lightning which can polarize your energy). The electromagnetic energy present in large stores and other public places—including radar, microwaves, cell phones, televisions and other electronic devices; sonar and magnetic imaging in medical use; and HARP and other tracking devices—scrambles our energy flow patterns. The Energy Band and Vortex can rebalance your electromagnetic energy and recharge and reset your energy flow pattern.

The first step in working with any system of energy balancing is to develop your perception of thoughts and energy.

Thoughts and Energy

Presently, humans are in a process of dimensional expansion. Since the Harmonic Convergence in 1987, our energy has been expanding into other dimensions where we can more fully experience universal life. It seems like every few months since the year 2000, our planet has undergone a major energy shift that affects our physical body in terms of health and life situations, and our energy body in terms of opening awareness and spiritual growth. In 2012, a Golden Doorway opened to let even more Universal Light Energy onto the planet, transforming all life by triggering spiritual growth and DNA adaptations. Mother Earth's heartbeat has changed its rhythm and we are changing our personal rhythm too, shifting gears as we enter a new dimension of existence. We are losing our physical density. Thoughts are quickening, emotions intensifying, and manifestation is immediate. As the Earth changes progress, humans are becoming more aware of our energy body and the true connection we have with the rest of life and this planet. Our perceptions continue to expand as we recognize that we share a common energy, a global mind, and the Universal Spirit of Life. We are energy beings envisioning our potential.

Just as we perceive images through our eyes and sound through our ears, we perceive energy through our thoughts and feelings. Every thought which enters our Energy Web, whether our own or someone else's, has the potential to manifest in our physical reality because thoughts move energy to create a physical form with the same characteristics as our thought vibration. If we carry a stress related thought or feeling in our Energy Web long enough, and nourish it through perpetuating that thought or feeling, then eventually it will enter our physical body through the weakest area and manifest as pain. For example, if we have a stressed-out day at work, and are sitting in traffic feeling this stress along with our thoughts of impatience, we may return home with a very sore neck and shoulders, possibly a headache as well. Our thoughts have entered through the place where we carry stress, then pain manifests as muscle tension. In this case, our weakest area is our tense neck and shoulders. By the same process, people develop cancer, ulcers, heart disease and many other illnesses. It is just as easy to manifest Unconditional Love, Universal Truth and Peace in our physical body and in our life. Each moment brings a choice for what we will manifest. All we need to do is change our thoughts and be willing to let go of old patterns.

If we take the same situation and carry positive thoughts in our Energy Web, we can easily recognize the introduction of stress related thoughts and choose to gently release or transform them. In this instance, we manifest calmness and strength that enters our physical body through our breath and heartbeat, manifesting health and well being. Suppose we have a stressed out day at work and are sitting in traffic feeling this stress along with thoughts of impatience. We can recognize the tension building in our neck and shoulders and realize that we are carrying stress from earlier events. At that moment, we can choose to let go of the stress and impatience. At the next stoplight, we take five slow, deep breaths. As we breathe, we let go of that energy and replace it with harmonious peaceful thoughts. Now we can return home feeling more at ease. We have brought our energy back into our Vibrational Light Center by releasing the thoughts that we do not want to manifest.

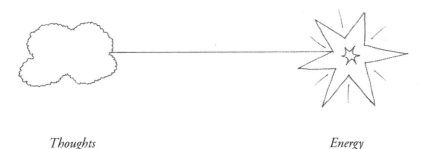

Thoughts   *Energy*

Thoughts and energy exist on a continuum. At one end of the continuum are our thoughts. Do you ever wonder where your thoughts come from? Most people assume that they have total control over what they think. However, since our thoughts are part of our Energy Web, we find that the energy we are carrying around—whether our own or influenced by others such as family, peers or society—becomes part of our thoughts. This process occurs without our conscious realization. As those thoughts stay in our Energy Web, they go on to influence our energy vibration and attract physical manifestations through the magnetism of like vibration. If those thoughts are destructive and they stay long enough in our Energy Web, they may make us feel depressed and eventually manifest as dysfunction in our physical body. However, once we become familiar with the thought patterns that are affecting a particular situation in our life, we can change those thoughts. Once our thoughts change, they influence our energy with a more positive vibration and attract new physical manifestations of well being and health. In this way, what we think really does create our physical reality, including personal health, relationships with others, and the environment.

At the other end of the continuum are our Spirit Essence (our vibrational light energy) and the guiding voice of our Guardian Spirit. Here we can perceive with our inner eyes and hear with our inner ears. The messages that we receive from our Guardian Spirit often seem like thoughts because they are interpreted the same way by our brain. However, we can also feel the energy behind these messages in our heart. A feeling of warmth, comfort, recognition, or excitement experienced deep within our Vibrational Light Center confirms the Truth behind the Spirit messages. Sometimes thoughts may be mistaken for Spirit messages and Spirit messages mistaken for thoughts. The more time we spend listening to our Spirit Essence and Guardian Spirit, the easier it becomes to distinguish their messages from the mindless thought stream that continually runs through our awareness. To be able to perceive at both ends of the energy/thought continuum, we must remain open to perceive the voice of our Guardian Spirit and develop the ability to shape our thoughts so that we create, rather than react, to life.

The Vortex works with Fifth World energy to allow our energy to expand into the Fifth, Sixth and Seventh Dimensions and beyond. In the Fifth World, we recognize our potential as creators. We know that thoughts create not only our personal reality; our collective thoughts affect the creatures, plants and trees, water, air, climate and Earth conditions as well. Just as we have created challenges for this planet, we can also manifest solutions for positive change and growth. In the Fifth World, we must take responsibility for all of our thoughts and actions and consider the repercussions of our choices on All Our Relations in the Web of Life.

The most important survival tool that we have at this time is Positive Thinking. Our positive thoughts can radiate out, like ripples on a pond, to create a healthy, peaceful planet. Positive thoughts also give us a solid foundation for doing Vortex Energy work, for with a good attitude we are ready to accept the changes that push us past our boundaries. When we recognize the good in something, we have unlimited potential, for we have recognized our true essence as Universal Beings. In preparation for using the Vortex, our thoughts must come from a place of Unconditional Love and we must plan every action to benefit the entire Earth Family for the next Seven Generations.

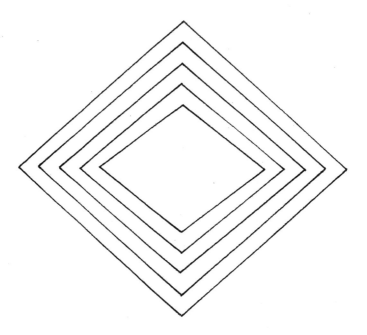

Preparing To Use The Vortex

"The diamond is the shape of the Vortex and the doorway to the Void. It represents the Universal Law of Transformation. As life continually recycles into new forms, the Vortex continually opens into the Void, where the potential exists to meet every possible need. The Vortex is also the doorway to other dimensions and allows our energy to expand and transform as our species evolves to adapt to future circumstances and environments. The Vortex holds the key for integrating body, mind and spirit into wholeness of being."

(From Grandmother Spider and the Web of Life by Spider)

The dictionary provides us with the following definition of Vortex applying to air and water:

"A whirling motion forming a vacuum cavity in the center. A whirlwind, rushing, absorbing and irresistible with catastrophic power."

When we visit a location where there is a naturally occurring Vortex, we can feel powerful swirling Vortex energy. There are many Vortexes on every continent on our planet; they are the places where Mother Earth breathes. At the Vortexes, energy from the Sun and other places in the Universe is drawn into the center of Mother Earth through her Energy Web and Mother Earth's energy is released back out through her connection to the Universal Web of Life. People and creature beings alike are attracted to Vortex locations by their electromagnetic pull. If we stay at a Vortex long enough, physical changes can, and do, manifest. This is evident when noticing that trees growing near a Vortex reflect the swirling energy in the formation of their branches and the way that the bark grows twisting up their trunks.

Earth Vortexes are sacred places. Through Earth Vortexes, we can directly connect to Mother Earth's Vibrational Light Center and reconnect our energy roots. As awakened creators, we humans have the responsibility to approach these special locations with an attitude of harmony and respect so that we can perpetuate the most balanced environment for the needs of all Mother Earth's Children. When we go to Vortex locations with chaotic or unclear thoughts, these are passed along to Mother Earth.

When we use the Vortex for our own personal evolution, we make a promise that we will also visit Mother Earth's Sacred Places and use our Vortex Energy there to replenish the planet. No matter where we live, we need not travel far to find Vortexes, for they are located in every area on the globe. As our perceptions awaken, we learn to recognize the Vortex centers in our own neighborhood.

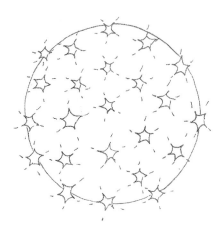

Earth's Vortex Energy Centers

We are beacons of energy, connecting the healing light energy of the Sky World with the nourishing foundation of the Earth World. Just as the Earth has special Vortex centers, so does our body. Our Energy Web breathes through our Vortex centers. Our Vortexes are the energy centers where we release imbalances in our electromagnetic field and attract replenishing energy from the Universe. We connect to the Web of Life and the environment around us through our Vortex Energy Centers.

Experiencing our Energy Web requires a special perception that each person learns to develop. It is more important that each person develop their own intuitive perception of the energy body surrounding themselves and others than to learn any one particular technique. It is essential to work with the thought/energy continuum and learn to distinguish and interpret your perceptions. Now that we are in the Fifth World, we learn through listening within. Each and every person can develop this talent. The Vortex work presented here assumes that the reader has some familiarity with energy perception. Please, take all the time you need to learn your own language of energy perception before you begin to work with creating the diamond Vortex. The Energy Band and Vertical Vortex are introductory exercises that are very helpful in perceiving the energy within our Energy Web.

We work in the Fifth Dimension when we create a Vortex. Although the Vortex works with the polarized energy flow between joints in the body, the Vortex does much more than encourages energy to flow along specific pathways. In the Vortex, we do not send energy or images to another person, or brush away energy that we feel is bad. When we create a Vortex, we simply acknowledge that we are energy beings who are part of the Grand Energy Field of the Universe and bring all energy pathways together so that the energy flow is harmonious. This occurs automatically, without our intention, when we put our hands together to create the diamond Vortex.

The Vortex is an alternative place outside of time, space and gravity, in which energy can easily rearrange by assuming new vibrations. Whatever is needed is brought from the Void through the doorway of the Vortex diamond and into form. It is precisely for this reason that the person using the Vortex is asked not to use intention. The Star People who have shared these teachings have made it clear that the Universe has a grand design and that using the Vortex opens up a pathway for that design to manifest.

We cannot assume that our own perception is best for manifesting the evolutionary changes for ourselves, another person, or even Mother Earth. Indeed, our personal perception may limit the possibilities of the Vortex. Therefore, once we create the Vortex, we give over to the Great Mystery and allow the Vortex Energy to do what it needs to do. We create the diamond Vortex, keep a clear, open mind, and allow the energy flow to happen without judgment or restriction. Trust that you will be guided during this process. Amazing things can happen for those who are sincerely ready to receive the abundance of the Universe.

Early in my Vortex experience, I learned first hand the reason why the Star People tell us not to use intention when using the Vortex. During an extended visit at a friend's house, I met a woman I will call Sue. About a week before I met Sue, she had twisted her ankle going down the basement steps. Since there were several wonderful healers in the area, Sue's ankle was taken care of with no problems. However, the day after I came to visit, Sue fell down the same step and twisted the same ankle in the same place. The injury was worse this second time around. I was the only person there that day and decided to use the Vortex to help Sue. I massaged the area of her foot that was twisted and swollen and we determined that the problem might have been where she was placing her foot while walking down the old cracked cement steps.

I opened up a diamond Vortex and placed the injured foot inside. I must admit a part of me wanted the swelling to go down and Sue's foot to feel better. But more than that, I wanted Sue to fully release the energy behind this situation that carried a message worth repeating. Then I heard the Star People, who were my teachers, telling me to keep my thoughts clear and just let the Vortex Energy work. I focused my thoughts on Unconditional Love and released expectations. A short while later, Sue remarked that she felt the Vortex Energy traveling up into her back. She shifted position and her back adjusted itself: we both heard it pop. Neither of us would have guessed that the problem was really in her back. Had I used intention, or even directed the Vortex solely to Sue's foot, I would have limited the transformation available to her through the Vortex. Since then, I have always used the Vortex without intention or direction, and have seen many wonderful and surprising things happen as a result.

Through the Vortex, we create an energy field with expanded vibrations, affecting the person creating it as well as the person, creature, plant, or location that is placed inside the Vortex doorway. Each time we use the Vortex, our energy expands. Therefore, it is wise to proceed slowly and allow energy changes to happen at a comfortable rate. The personal exercises presented here are important because they prepare your energy to be able to use the Vortex, and thus assist with your own evolutionary process. Take your time, observe how these exercises change your energy flow, and then watch how this different energy flow manifests in your life.

When we work with another person, we realize that we cannot heal or change their chosen lessons; we can only present the opportunity for that person to release, renew and make new choices. Of course, the other person probably will not consciously know what is best for their evolution, so both people need to remain of clear mind and without intent during the Vortex process. These Vortex exercises enable us to assist others in their evolutionary growth at a speed that is totally comfortable for them.

When we use the Vortex, we are responsible for giving the energy back to Mother Earth by creating group Vortex Energy circles. As we create the Fifth World, the next step in evolution is for small groups to come together to create a Common Mind in preparation for awakening the Planetary Mind. Working with the Vortex strengthens group bonding as well as allows Mother Earth the opportunity for growth and change.

The Star People gave the information for Vortex transformation to Spider over a two-year period. These people from Lyre have developed Vortex knowledge according to Universal Laws and they are committed to helping us remember these skills that our Ancient Ancestors once used. The Star People tell us that each step in this process is very important and should be worked with for several weeks before going on to the next lesson. A thorough knowledge of each step is essential for creating and activating the Vortex doorway. As explained earlier, you will develop your own way of perceiving energy through your intuitive senses. The more you work with energy, the more your awareness and vibration will shift. Please, take your time and trust your inner voice.

The effective use of the Vortex requires that we approach these techniques while anchored within the Truth of our Vibrational Light Center—which is honoring our personal Medicine Wheel, our Earth Connection and our purpose for this Earth Walk. We only approach the Vortex through sharing thoughts of Unconditional Love, and with the motivation for creating peace. We stand in trust, without using any particular intention; knowing that through this doorway, our Energy Web will connect with the Universal Energy Field and bring balance to every part of our being.

Every time we use the Vortex, we move further along in evolution: our body actually changes dimension. As we work, we weave awake the vibration of Universal Awareness that connects all creature beings in the Web of Life. The Vortex activates our star energy, opening us up as a conduit of energy transference between the Earth and the Universe and reaching out to reconnect with the Web of Life. The Vortex leads us back to the unity of energy within the Great Energy Field of the Great Mystery—the completion of the process of growth that is our reason for existence.

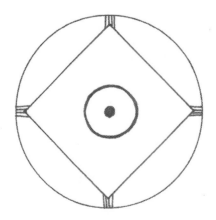

PART FOUR: VORTEX EXERCISES

One of the reasons the Star People have given us the Vortex knowledge at this time is so we can expand our personal vibrations and evolve with the Fifth World energy and environment. Each time we use the Vortex, our energy expands. We never return to our original state of energy and we remain changed as a result of our experience. The more Vortex work we do, the more our energy changes. This energy change manifests as balance within our life. The results of expanded Vortex Energy include: clear perception; alignment with Universal Wisdom; manifestation of our needs; personal health; improved relationships based on attracting others with similar vibrations; adaptation to our changing external environment; and the ability to experience the Fifth Dimension and higher dimensions.

The Star People have taught us several ways to use the Vortex on ourselves to align and expand our energy. If we use the Vortex Energy exercises for personal balance on a regular basis, we will be more effective in using the Vortex to assist others in balancing themselves. We can best survive Earth and environmental changes by focusing our energy through the Personal Vortex.

Personal Vortex Work

A Vortex is an energy space that rearranges every aspect of our existence. It affects the very essence of our being, aligning us with our role in the Universal Dance of Life. The Energy Web of the Universe is made up of Vortexes. We enter and exit our Earth Walk through Vortex Ladders. When we are in a Vortex, we align our Energy Web with the Universal Energy Web. Healing occurs within our physical and emotional bodies and is reflected in our personal relationships and situation in the world.

We can create a Vortex Energy field through specific placement of our hands, connecting the two polar fields of our body to create an Energy Band. The left side of our body is the side where we receive energy and has a negative electromagnetic charge (-). The right side of our body is where we give away energy and has a positive electromagnetic charge (+). When these negative/positive (or nourishing/releasing) poles are connected, they create a strong energy flow. It is within this Energy Band that we establish an environment for healing through transforming energy.

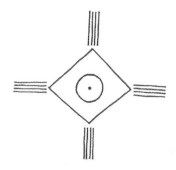

Exercise 1: Creating an Energy Band

The Energy Band polarizes, or electromagnetically aligns, your Energy Web. The dictionary gives this definition of Polarization: A condition of light or radiant heat in which the transverse vibrations of the rays assume different forms in different planes.

As it applies to Vortex Energy, polarization can be achieved by using a magnetic Energy Band created with your hands. Begin simply by standing or sitting straight, with both feet flat on the floor, and place your hands together with all the corresponding finger joints touching. This is the most balanced position that you can assume. Due to the opposing magnetic charges of each hand, the Energy Band creates a strong magnetic pull that affects your entire Energy Web and your physical body on the cellular level. When you draw the Energy Band down your physical body, the energy (light) vibrations balance cell structure and align the physical and energy bodies. When you turn your hand positions using Reverse Polarity, you are working in a different energetic plane. That energy plane shift creates opportunities to manifest changes in our Energy Web and physical form. Polarization removes blocks within energy flow patterns, awakens memory (both remembering our past and our purpose), and activates the new energy flow patterns of the Fifth World.

Polarization using the Energy Band and Vortex will align your body with Fifth Dimensional energy. You will feel physical and emotional changes; however, these may be very subtle. Allow yourself to experience each exercise fully and then practice each for as long as it takes to integrate your system. Please proceed at your own pace.

Select a private place where you can work without distraction. Stand with your feet about shoulder width apart. Begin by putting your hands together, fingertips pointing towards the sky. Make sure that the corresponding joints on each hand are directly touching each other. Hold your hands in this position for a few minutes. Take five slow, deep breaths to draw your awareness back into your Vibrational Light Center. It is no mystery that this is also the position of prayer. When we connect our hands, we balance our energy and can connect with the Universal Mind, the Great Mystery, the Source of Being.

As previously explained, the left side of the body has a negative charge and the right side a positive charge. We create a strong electromagnetic field when we put our hands together to connect the two energy charges. This is similar to putting together the opposing ends of two magnets.

The energy flowing between them tends to push the two apart. This energy flow of attraction/resistance sets up a vibrational pattern that can polarize our energy. We prepare to work with Vortex energy by using the Energy Band to polarize our energy. The Energy Band brings personal energy into a harmonious vibration and shifts our dimensional reality.

Both sides of your body have distinct rhythms. Feel the rhythm on the left side of your body and notice how energy moves there. Think about how you relate to that energy flow. The left side of the body is your receiving side and your left hand brings in energy to nourish body, mind and spirit. Check in and see how your energy is flowing on your left side.

Now feel the rhythm on the right side of your body. This is the releasing side of the body where you give away energy. Check in and see how your energy is flowing on your right side. How is the movement of energy different on the right side compared to the left side? Notice how the energy flows on the two sides of your body are different and similar at the same time.

It is normal for each side of the body to have a distinct rhythm of energy. Sometimes the two rhythms are very different from each other. If you wish to explore these rhythms separately, first focus on the left side of your body and feel the rhythm there. Allow that rhythm to take over your entire body and move with that rhythm in a dance of receiving energy. When you have finished this dance, rest a few minutes, and then do the same thing on the right side of your body: focus on the rhythm of the right side of your body, and then create a dance of giving away energy that you can experience through your entire body.

After you have checked in with both sides of your body, bring your hands together again with all the joints of your fingers touching. Allow your energy to begin flowing out of the joints of your right hand and through the joints of your left hand. Feel the energy flow into your left hand, circulate throughout your body, and then return to your right hand where it flows once again into your left hand and continues with this circular energy flow pattern. Allow the energy to flow between your hands until they create one unified rhythm on both sides of your body. Now you have created your personal circle of harmony.

After you feel the energy from both sides of your body flowing together as one unified rhythm, slowly begin to separate your hands. Move in very slow motion. As you pull your fingers apart, feel the Energy Band extending from the joints in one hand to the corresponding joints in the opposite hand. It resembles the feeling of pulling long, sticky threads of taffy. Let your hands act on their own, without thinking about it, and separate them just as far as you feel comfortable. Some people have described this as feeling like they have an energy balloon inflated between their hands. You have now created the Energy Band.

Making an Energy Band is the first step in polarizing your energy. Energy flows from joint to joint throughout your physical body. Each joint is a small Vortex center where energy flows into and out of your body. When you put your hands together, you set up an energy field with a very strong magnetic flow. You can visualize this magnetic energy flow as a band of energy moving between your hands. This Energy Band creates an environment for your energy to line up, which in turn creates an environment for the molecules and atoms in your body to line up. The Energy Band erases blockages in your Energy Web, harmonizes your vibration, and changes the magnetic programming of the cells within its field.

You can direct the Energy Band by moving your hands over your body. Move both of your hands at the same time, so that the magnetic energy flow remains intact, and place them over your head as far up as you can reach. Separate your hands a little so that you can fit your head inside the Energy Band. Slowly bring your hands down to your shoulders. You should feel the magnetic pull of the Energy Band as you go. The slower you move, the better opportunity for the Energy Band to balance and polarize your energy. If you lose this feeling, you can go back to create the Energy Band and start over again.

The Energy Band balances your energy much like turning the dial on the radio eliminates the static. As the Energy Band travels, it changes the vibration of discordant energy and pulls energy that has been scattered back into your Vibrational Light Center. This brings a sense of inner harmony and strengthens your Universal Wisdom Pathway. Continuing down your body, move your hands further apart so that your body will fit inside the Energy Band. Slowly move the Energy Band all the way to your feet. You can either bend down to your feet or hold your hands in position as far as they will go and visualize the Energy Band continuing down to your feet.

To close off the Energy Band, gently release your feet from the Energy Band and then bring your hands back up to the front of your body. Your hands should be about 8 or 10 inches apart. Slowly bring your hands together until all the joints touch.

I like to do the Energy Band at night before I go to bed as it leaves me with a grounded, peaceful energy. The magnetic alignment of the Energy Band harmonizes all that has happened during the day, bringing a closure and leaving me ready to rest before beginning again in the morning.

Practice creating the Energy Band with a partner. Although it is not possible to do a whole body Energy Band for another person, you can use the Energy Band on a specific area. To do this, make the Energy Band the same as before, allowing your own energy to come into balance, and then place your hands on either side of your partner's head. Listen to your own Language of Perception as you experience the Energy Band polarization. Notice how your perception of energy changes when you interact with someone else's energy field. Do not attempt to direct this energy, just let it flow. When learning the Language of Energy Perception, it is especially important to have an exchange of partner feedback, so take time to share your perceptions and listen to your partner's experience. That way you can verify both your perceptions and the response of the person experiencing your work.

Exercise 2: Reverse Polarity

After you use the Energy Band to polarize your energy, your vibration is aligned and you experience a strong directional energy flowing through your Energy Web and the energy pathways that travel through your physical body. If you suddenly reverse the direction of the polarized energy field, the polarities change and cause the electromagnetic energy of your body's cells to pull in two directions instead of only one. Cells are most vulnerable to change when a new energy pattern establishes flow after the old energy flow is abruptly unsupported. The electromagnetic energy within the cells becomes unstable for an instant—long enough for the charge to change and the energy to begin flowing in a different pattern. The new energy pattern always reflects whatever the electromagnetic field and the body's cells need at this time. I call this process of reversing the direction of an energy field Reverse Polarity. Reverse Polarity resets the body's electromagnetic energy flow.

To experience Reverse Polarity, set up the Energy Band just as you did before. Once you can feel the energy flowing between your hands, widen them a little bit and place your hands on either side of your ears. Allow yourself to experience the energy flow pattern of this Energy Band. Your Sensory Centers are the most sensitive places in your body, so you can easily feel the energy vibrations. Notice how your energy is flowing.

When your energy perception is clear, turn your hands a quarter turn so that your right hand is in front of your forehead and your left hand is behind the nape of your neck. (I usually always move in a counterclockwise direction; however there have been times when I was lead to move in a clockwise direction—follow your intuitive feelings.) Perceive this new energy flow. Have no expectations; just observe how the energy has changed. When you are ready, close off the Energy Band the same as before by bringing your hands slowly back together.

You can use the Energy Band and Reverse Polarity on any part of your body. Experiment with areas that are injured or painful and notice what happens.

You can also use Reverse Polarity on your entire body. Simply make the Energy Band as you did in the previous exercise. Start at the top of your head and slowly move the Energy Band down below your feet. When you have gone as far as you can go, turn your hands a quarter turn so that your right hand is in front of your feet and your left hand behind. Slowly draw your hands back up to the top of your head. You will have to stop for a moment around your shoulders and move your left hand into position to continue moving upward. When you have finished, close off the Energy Band as before. Take a moment to notice how your energy vibration has changed.

Practice Reverse Polarity with a partner. Although it is not possible to do a whole body Reverse Polarity on someone else, you can work on a problem area or on one of the Vortex Energy centers. The place where we perceive energy most clearly is our Sensory Centers. Create an Energy Band and place it over the Sensory Centers, positioning one hand on either side of the ears. When you feel the energy flowing strongly between your hands, turn your hands a quarter turn so that your right hand is in front of the face and your left hand behind the head. Notice what changes occur in the energy flow after you shift your hands. Exchange feedback with your partner to see how they perceived the Reverse Polarity energy shift.

Again, it is essential not to direct this energy with our thoughts. We have created an energy space that allows our physical body to manifest whatever changes our electromagnetic field and physical structure require. Although we may think we know where the energy should be directed, often there are very subtle multidimensional influences that are beyond our understanding or perception. Since we cannot assume what our Energy Web or cells require, and we surely cannot know the needs of another person, we only limit our work if we allow our mind to enter the process. It's best to give over and trust that what is truly needed will happen.

Practice the Energy Band on yourself at least a dozen times before going on to the next exercise. Each time you use the Energy Band, your vibrations will slightly shift. Over time, you will notice a difference in your magnetic energy, your energy level, and the things that manifest in your life. It is essential to develop a thorough knowledge of each step of this process in order to effectively use Vortex Energy.

The Vertical Vortex

Exercise 3: The Vertical Vortex

The Vertical Vortex opens up the energy flow through your Universal Wisdom Pathway, the energy pathway that flows from the Earth up through your feet, straight up through your body, and out the top of your head into the Universe. When your Universal Wisdom Pathway is open, you become an energy channel from Mother Earth to the Universal Mind. The Vertical Vortex is an important step in preparing to create the Vortex, for you can only do Vortex Energy work when your Universal Wisdom Pathway is open.

Before you can work with the Vortex, you need to prepare your energy. It is essential that you be anchored in Truth awareness (maintain a sincere, positive, peaceful attitude), because the Vortex opens a doorway for all possibilities to manifest. Since the Vertical Vortex opens the energy flow through your Universal Wisdom Pathway, you can use it to prepare by clearing your Universal Wisdom Pathway on a regular basis. When your Universal Wisdom Pathway is clear, you have the ability to manifest easily and quickly. If you are not anchored in Truth awareness, you are not in alignment with Universal Wisdom. Under these circumstances, your energy may be scattered and prevent you from accessing Vortex energy. It is unwise to use the Vortex until you have opened your Universal Wisdom Pathway.

The Vertical Vortex is a personal exercise that should be used daily to open up your Universal Wisdom Pathway. This simple exercise is so effective that I have heard stories from students, who during a stressful day at work excused themselves to go to the bathroom for a private space to do the Vertical Vortex so that they could remain centered.

The Vertical Vortex acts as a magnet to center your energy. During the experiences of your day, you give away energy. Some energy is pulled ahead of you, maybe even way outside the boundary of your Energy Web, thinking of future concerns. Some energy is pulled out behind you, concerned with unfinished business from the past. Energy is also pulled out to either side of your body, supporting the expectations of different relationships and maybe even taking on the responsibilities of another person. The magnetic vibration of the Vertical Vortex gently brings your energy back into balance within your Vibrational Light Center. You feel centered and grounded, fully present with the concerns of the moment, standing solidly on the Earth.

When used daily, the Vertical Vortex adjusts your personal vibration so that it becomes easier to work with Vortex energy. It opens up your perception of energy within the more expanded dimensions that we all experience as we evolve into the Fifth World of Unity. This simple tool is the most effective knowledge we have to integrate the evolutionary leap of energy that our planet is now undergoing.

Making The Vertical Vortex

To start the Vertical Vortex, begin with an Energy Band at your Vibrational Light Center, right above your navel. Let the Energy Band rest for a few moments with your hands open, until you can feel the magnetic energy flow, and then bring your hands back together. Without breaking the physical contact between your hands, flip them over sideways so that your right hand is on top and your left hand on the bottom. Now your fingers will be facing opposite directions while your palms remain touching. Slowly raise your right hand straight up. Let your right hand go as far as it feels comfortable. Your left hand will stay at your Vibrational Light Center. You can always mentally extend the Vertical Vortex past the location where your hand can reach. When your right hand is raised, you are opening up a pathway to the Universal Mind. Stay in this position as long as you need to center energy on your Universal Wisdom Pathway. Then bring your right hand back down to touch palms again with your left hand.

Without breaking the physical contact between your hands, flip them over so that your left hand is on top and your right hand on the bottom. Once again, your palms will remain in contact while your fingers face in opposite directions. With your left hand remaining at your Vibrational Light Center, slowly extend your right hand down towards the Earth. Go as far as is comfortable. Again, you can always mentally extend the Vertical Vortex past the location where your right hand can reach. When your right hand is extended down, you are opening up a pathway to the heartbeat of Mother Earth. Stay here as long as necessary to center your energy on your Universal Wisdom Pathway.

When you are finished, bring your right hand back up to touch palms with your left hand. Without breaking contact, flip your hands so that your palms remain touching and your fingers are facing in the same direction, connecting joint to joint, pointing towards the sky. This is the original hand position where we started the Energy Band. Take a few moments to feel how your energy has changed since you brought your energy back into your Universal Wisdom Pathway. To complete the Vertical Vortex, turn your palms into your Vibrational Light Center and seal the Vertical Vortex within, right hand over your left hand, with the thumbs touching each other.

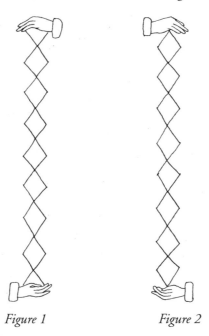

Figure 1   *Figure 2*

The geometric energy flow pattern of the Vertical Vortex is a series of diamonds connected together in a line between your hands. When your right hand is on top, extending upwards, the diamonds on the ends are open to receive energy. (Figure 1) Your energy is open and expanding, aligning with the Universal Mind and the Great Energy Field. When your right hand is on the bottom, extending downwards, the diamonds on the ends are closed. (Figure 2) Your energy is grounded into the foundation of the Earth. Both of these pathways of the Vertical Vortex magnetize our Universal Wisdom Pathway.

The Vertical Vortex can only be used on yourself. You can create the Vertical Vortex to magnetize your Universal Wisdom Pathway and the other Truth Lines in your body but it is not possible to extend these same energy flow patterns to another person in exactly the same way because each of us has a different energy vibration. The Star People gave us the Vertical Vortex so that we could adapt our personal energy vibration to the changing energy of the Earth by strengthening our individual Universal Wisdom Pathway.

It is essential to do the Vertical Vortex daily to align your Truth energy within your Vibrational Light Center before you can go on to use the diamond Vortex. Practice the Energy Band and the Vertical Vortex for at least two weeks before going further. Make a mental notation of how your energy and perception changes as you use the Vertical Vortex. Keep in mind that events occurring in our environment trigger energy changes. If appropriate, you may want to keep a journal. Remember, there is no such thing as a coincidence!

Exercise 4: Aligning Your Truth Lines

This Vortex session is done using the Vertical Vortex to align the Truth Lines in your body. This is a great way to nourish yourself and get your energy moving. Using the Vertical Vortex on the Truth Lines strengthens your personal vibration and increases the energy flow patterns through your body between the Earth and the Universe. This exercise is balancing and reenergizing. You can do this everyday.

Remember not to use any particular intention while working with the Vortex. We do not wish to limit the extent of the balancing that we can achieve. Just relax, keep your thoughts in your body and in the present moment, and allow yourself to open up to the Unconditional Love of the Universe.

Stand with your feet a comfortable distance apart, about the width of your shoulders. Place your hands on your Vibrational Light Center, right over left. Breathe five times to align your energy, then unfold your hands and place your palms and all finger joints together. Flip your hands over so that the right hand is on top, fingers pointing in opposite directions. You are now prepared to do the Vertical Vortex. In this exercise, you are going to do rows of Vertical Vortexes along the Truth Lines.

Hold each Vertical Vortex as long as is comfortable, and then come back to place your palms and all the joints of your fingers together before beginning a new Vertical Vortex. Always begin on the left side, where we bring nourishment into our body.

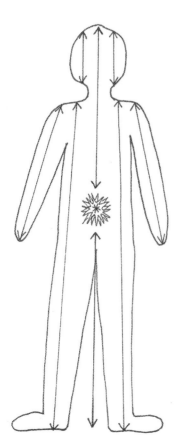

For these Vertical Vortexes, your right hand will be on top.

1. Left shoulder to palm of left hand.

2. Left shoulder to top of head, left side.

3. Left shoulder to left hip.

4. Left hip to bottom of left foot.

5. Your Vibrational Light Center to the top of your head.

For these Vertical Vortexes, your left hand will be on top.

6. Flip your hands over and go from your Vibrational Light Center to below your feet.

7. Right shoulder to top of head, right side.

8. Right shoulder to right hip.

9. Right hip to bottom of right foot.

10. Right shoulder to palm of right hand.

Exercise 5: Aligning Your Memory Lines

The Memory Line pathways flow from both sides of your body through your Universal Wisdom Pathway like a series of X's beginning in the Energy Web above your head and ending in the Energy Web below your feet. You can align the energy flow along your Memory Lines using an Energy Band. This is a good exercise to do after aligning your Truth Lines, as energy flowing through your Memory Lines energizes cellular energy flow, triggers DNA, and helps maintain physical balance.

Make an Energy Band at the center of the Memory Line cross. Pull your hands apart and keep them facing each other. Place them in position A of step one listed below. Hold the Energy Band until you feel the energy shift. Then bring your hands back together in the center of the Memory Line cross and open another Energy Band, placing it in position B. Bring your hands back together, place them in the center of the next Memory Line cross and repeat the steps above. This exercise can be done standing or sitting.

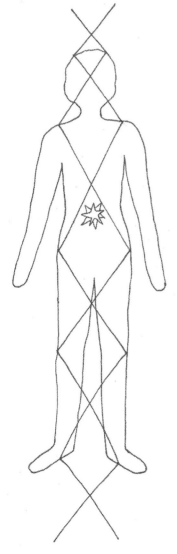

1. **Memory Line Cross in Energy Web Above Head:**

     A. Right hand in Energy Web; Left hand on left top of head.

     B. Left hand in Energy Web; Right hand on right top of head.

2. **Memory Line Cross Sensory Center (In front of nose):**

     A. Right hand on right top of head; Left hand on left shoulder.

     B. Left hand on left top of head; Right hand on right shoulder.

3. **Memory Line Cross at Heart Center:**

     A. Right hand on right shoulder; Left hand on left hip.

     B. Left hand on left shoulder; Right hand on right hip.

4. **Memory Line Cross at Reproductive Center:**

     A. Right hand on right hip; Left hand on left knee.

     B. Left hand on left hip; Right hand on right knee.

5. **Memory Line Cross at Calves:**

     A. Right hand on right knee; Left hand on left foot.

     B. Left hand on left knee; Right hand on right foot.

6. **Memory Line Cross at Feet:**

     A. Right hand on right foot; Left hand extended below left foot in Energy Web.

     B. Left hand on left foot; Right hand extended below right foot in Energy Web.

Exercise 6: Creating the Vortex

Vortex: *A doorway to wholeness, filled with non-judgmental energy, giving high respect to that which has beauty. A measuring of possibilities for the future. The opening to other dimensions of existence.*

As previously stated, in order to open the doorway of the Vortex, you must first align your Energy Web and bring your awareness into your Vibrational Light Center. By this time, you should feel very comfortable working with the Energy Band. The Vortex is created in exactly the same way. To begin creating the Vortex, take all the steps of bringing your energy into wholeness; take five deep breaths, create the Energy Band, and polarize your energy. Be sure to include all of the steps. This entire process is necessary to actualize the Vortex Energy. It is not necessary to Reverse Polarity or do the Vertical Vortex before creating the diamond Vortex.

When you place your hands together, you create a very strong magnetic field. That's why you can feel the magnetism pulling from joint to joint when you pull your hands apart. You have already experienced the effects of this strong magnetic field when you polarized your energy. If you hold your hands in this position for a while, the energy flowing between your hands will line up to form an energy Vortex. The energy flow pattern of the Vortex is the shape of a diamond, an octahedron, or double pyramid.

It works something like this. Energy molecules are present in a fairly evenly spaced energy pattern around any physical body. Even though these energy molecules are in constant motion, they keep their general magnetic spacing pattern, or flow pattern. When we have an area of our body that holds pain or resistance, or when we reverse the polarity, this energy pattern changes and becomes an irregular placement of energy molecules. If we stay long enough in the Energy Band, we can create an irregular electromagnetic energy pattern. In this case, many energy molecules concentrate at the strongest point, forming the shape of the diamond between your hands, while other energy particles are electromagnetically repelled and scatter outward in circular forms surrounding the Vortex diamond.

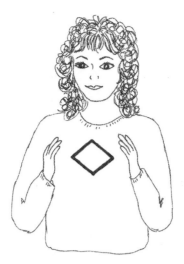

The Diamond Vortex Lines up Between Your Hands

When you created the Energy Band, the energy flow felt as though you were pulling taffy. Energy flowed from the joints of one hand directly across to the corresponding joints of the other hand. After you stay in this energy field awhile, the energy molecules begin to magnetize and start to line up where the energy field has the most magnetic attraction. This is the place directly centered between your palms.

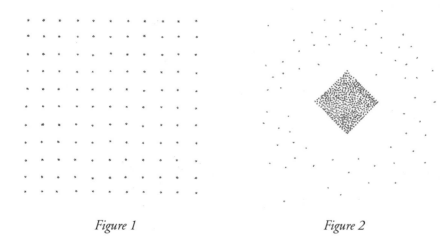

Figure 1   *Figure 2*

Figure 1 shows a hypothetical version of the energy pattern of molecules. As the electromagnetic attraction between your hands increases, the energy lines up something like the placement of molecules in Figure 2. A dense pattern of concentrated energy molecules forms in the central location—the diamond—while the remaining energy molecules spread out to form an arc, which is considerably finer in density, around the energy Vortex. The energy flow pattern changes as the energy from the joints of one hand now connect to the opposite joints of the other hand. For example, the energy from the top joint of your first right finger will connect with the wrist joint directly below the little finger of your left hand. If you take pieces of thread and physically recreate this pattern, you will find a diamond made of eight sides where all the energy lines intersect. You will see a diamond if you look between your hands, as in Figure 3, and you will also see a diamond if you look down on your hands.

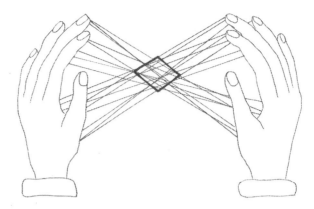

Figure 3—Creating The Diamond Vortex

The diamond is the focus of Vortex Energy; it becomes so concentrated with energy molecules that it forms an electromagnetic energy beam comparable to a laser beam. When working with the diamond Vortex, we use the Vortex energy beam to make changes that can result in healing and positive growth for ourselves, other people, animals, plants and even the Earth. The effects of Vortex Energy always reach far from our hands, extending out to bring transformation to many others who are not directly connected to our work.

To experience the Vortex, begin at your Vibrational Light Center. Place your left hand on your Vibrational Light Center and put your right hand over it. Take five slow, deep breaths. Slowly unfold your hands and put your palms together with fingertips touching. Now pull your hands apart, create the Energy Band, and go through the same process of clearing your energy just as you have previously done with the Energy Band. Relax.

Now, bring your hands back in front of your Vibrational Light Center and hold them about 8-10 inches apart. Focus your perceptions on the space between your hands and feel the energy line up to form the diamond Vortex. (It may take some practice, but you will be able to perceive the shift in energy flow.) If you have a difficult time perceiving the energy shift, bring your hands back together after completing the Energy Band, fingers touching joint to joint, take another deep breath, then slowly separate your hands and let Vortex form. Allow the diamond image to become strong and clear. Put yourself into the diamond and sit in the doorway. Keep you thoughts clear and focused on Unconditional Love. If any other thoughts come into your mind, allow them to be released into the Vortex.

Visualize Yourself Inside The Diamond Vortex

The first way that we can work with the diamond Vortex is to simply visualize a clear image inside of the diamond using our thoughts. We can place ourselves, a specific situation, another person, or even the Earth inside the Vortex. The diamond is a doorway to the Universal Mind. Keep in mind that you are placing others or yourself in the Vortex without intention. While inside the Vortex, the person, place or situation has the opportunity to manifest changes because the Universal Mind provides for the highest vibrations of harmony to manifest at all times. Energy flow patterns literally rearrange to accommodate these new vibrations. Corresponding to the energy changes, our body can rearrange cell structure, a situation can change focus and intensity, and our planet can rearrange growth patterns to regenerate exhausted resources. Whatever we truly need will always manifest.

You can keep the diamond Vortex open for as long as you like. You may feel energy moving or pulsing, or experience other sensations while you have the Vortex open. Depending on how you perceive energy, what you sense may be totally different than what someone else senses. Everyone's experience is valid. The experience of the Vortex should be pleasant but it can also be intense. This is because Vortex Energy tends to speed things up. The Vortex hastens the healing process, which may cause uncomfortable feelings and releasing. It can also affect the weather, picking up the wind and rain. It's best to have a sensitive approach when using the Vortex and close it off at the right time. When it feels like you have been in the Vortex long enough, when the energy shifts, or when you begin to have trouble concentrating on the image, its time to close.

Because space, time, and energy are bound together in multi-dimensions, its important to close the Vortex while standing in the exact same location and position as you were when you opened the Vortex. To close the Vortex, return to your original position and gently release the image from inside the diamond. Then slowly bring your hands back together until all the joints of your fingers touch. It is a good idea to turn your hands over and do the Vertical Vortex at this time to center your energy on your Universal Wisdom Pathway. When you finish, turn your palms into your Vibrational Light Center so that you can seal the Vortex Energy inside.

Place The Diamond Vortex Around A Person, Creature, Plant or Location

Another way to use the Vortex diamond is to physically place something inside of the diamond. This can be done in a similar way to the process we used to create the Energy Band. We simply create the Vortex diamond and then place our hands over something. If you want to place yourself into the Vortex here's how you would do it: After you feel the Vortex diamond form, move your hands further apart, say a comfortable distance outside your physical body, then visualize the diamond Vortex enlarging and surrounding your entire body, as if you are standing inside the diamond. The size of the diamond will change depending on where you are working. If you have a headache for example, you can place one hand on either side of your head, placing the center of the diamond Vortex inside your head. I use this method when I work on another person to open up Vortex Energy Centers within the body and to help with healing. You can use the diamond Vortex on animals and plants as well.

You will feel the energy flow when you use the Vortex on someone, and this can give you an indication of what is happening with them. Sometimes people who use the Vortex on others feel the energy flow patterns within themselves as well. I often feel energy flowing through my own head, for example, when I work on someone else's head. The Vortex brings balance and healing for both of us. After you feel the energy shift, it is time to close the Vortex. Do this by visualizing the diamond between your hands and then slowly and gently pulling it out and away from their body. Bring your hands back in front of you, and then slowly bring your hands together until all the finger joints touch. Do the Vertical Vortex to center your energy.

Be aware that the Vortex opens a doorway for transformation but we cannot define what that transformation should be. In our society, our healers and doctors are presumed failures when the patient dies. However, if you realize that we chose our life lessons before we manifest our physical body, then we each have challenges and choices that define our state of health and how we will live. It is always wrong for us to try and change someone else's choices. In other words, we must not visualize a person recovering from injury or illness; it may not be a part of their path. We can send love to support them in whatever path they consciously or unconsciously choose at that time and let the Vortex Energy do the appropriate rearranging.

The Vortex connects energy vibrations that communicate instantaneously on many levels of our Energy Web and physical body. There are no communication barriers. Therefore, it is possible to communicate on the deepest nonverbal levels with animals, plants, stones and other people through the Vortex. This language is not the same as the language of words that is understood by our mind. Our words define and divide in their effort to describe and categorize the world around us. Vibrational communication through the Vortex is more easily understood through our heart and feelings. Feelings interpret energy vibrations through many senses located in your physical body and Energy Web. Most likely, you will understand the messages received through the Vortex but have a difficult time translating them into words. Vortex communication works both ways; this is the reason that it is necessary to keep our thoughts focused on sharing Unconditional Love and creating peace when using the Vortex.

I have seen some awesome things happen when working with the Vortex. There have been changes so small they were almost unnoticed, but left a permanent impact on the life of the person that I worked with, usually in the areas of personal relationships or health. In some instances, plants and trees that were dying regained their energy and began producing fruit the next year. I used the Vortex over time and saw a waste area slowly begin to regenerate into a healthy ecosystem.

There have also been instantaneous transformations that were apparent immediately after Vortex sessions. Sick and injured animals regained health after grim prognosis. People were able to release emotional attachments along with corresponding pain and physical limitations that they may have carried for many years. One woman, scheduled for surgery the next day, released a bowel obstruction. Four rows of corn in a garden sprouted and sent up shoots within twenty-four hours after planting followed by a group Vortex on the site.

There are many more examples of the energy changes brought about through the Vortex. One fact remains constant in determining the extent of energy shifting that the Vortex will have: The Vortex brings what we are willing to receive at that time. In every case the Vortex positively adjusts energy, bringing peace and harmony to everyone involved and the surrounding environment.

Remember, in all Vortex work, we never send intention into the diamond. In no instance are we able to determine consciously what is needed for healing ourself or another person. We may think that we know what is needed, but there are so many variables involved that we are not aware of. The Vortex is Fifth Dimension energy; therefore we must give our ego control over to the Great Mystery and trust that what occurs is the best gift that can manifest at this time. Otherwise, we not only limit the results of our Vortex work, but we limit the expansion of our personal vibration as well.

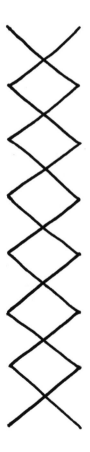

Exercise 7: Personal Vortex

We can use the diamond Vortex as a doorway for personal transformation. This exercise can be done sitting or standing, whatever is most comfortable for you. Prepare for this Vortex the same way that you do for the other Vortex exercises: Start with balancing the two sides of your body, create the Energy Band, and then polarize your energy. Bring your hands back up to create the diamond Vortex. Let the diamond expand to become larger than your two hands, large enough to encompass your entire body. All of your Sacred Space-your physical body, your Energy Web, your thoughts and emotions-will be inside the Vortex.

Remember, just allow yourself to be inside the Vortex doorway, do not place an intention inside the Vortex. Your conscious awareness may not know what is best for you at this time. Trust that you are being guided to receive exactly what you need. If you attempt to define or direct the energy of the Vortex, you will only limit the scope of possibilities. If you know your healing color, or your healing sound, you can place it inside the diamond with you to align your experience with your personal vibration. You can stay in the Vortex as long as you like.

While inside the Vortex, you may feel energy moving or other specific sensations. Keep your thoughts clear, without definition or expectation, and allow the transformations to happen. If you get persistent distracting thoughts, bring your mind back to focus on your breathing, the rhythm of your heartbeat, your healing color, or your healing sound. The Vortex may bring strong energy flow patterns but it should not be painful. If the Vortex experience does not feel right to you in any way, close off the diamond Vortex and try again at another time.

I have discovered that there are times when the Energy Web of the planet is unstable and I have been prevented from opening a Vortex at these times. There are magnetic storms and vibrational fluctuations that interfere with the Vortex. These are not frequent occurrences, but are conditions outside of us that directly affect the Vortex experience. I have been told by the Star People to refrain from using the Vortex at these times. As you become more sensitive to energy, you will perceive when conditions are not receptive.

When you feel ready, or when you feel the energy shift, gently release yourself from the Vortex and bring your hands back together in front of your Vibrational Light Center. Turn your palms over and energize your Universal Wisdom Pathway with the Vertical Vortex. It's best to allow some time to yourself after working with Vortex Energy so that the transformation can expand and integrate on all levels of your being. The Vortex puts you in a different dimension, and if you move too quickly you can become rather disoriented.

Exercise 8: Vortex Meditation

We can use the diamond Vortex to access Universal Wisdom and learn the answers to questions. Select a quiet time and location and find a comfortable sitting position, either on the floor or in a chair. Start with balancing the energy between the two sides of your body, create an Energy Band, and polarize your energy. Bring your hands in front of your Vibrational Light Center and create the diamond Vortex. Allow the diamond to expand and become larger than your hands—large enough to encompass your physical body and Energy Web. Sit for a few minutes and allow the energy of your breathing to become harmonious.

Create a second diamond Vortex with your hands and allow it to enlarge so that your body and Energy Web are also inside this Vortex. Now you are sitting in a Vortex within a Vortex. Take a moment to feel this energy shift, and then let your mind focus on your question. Be as clear as you can with your question, because if you are confused when you ask the question, your answer may be confused. You do not have to ask just yes-and-no questions. It is all right to ask, "How can I do this?" or "What does this mean?" Your energy perception will open up to understand choices based on Universal Wisdom and universal Laws. You can also visualize an image if it is appropriate for your question. For example, if you are asking about healing a part of your body, visualize that part of your body where you are experiencing dis-ease or pain. By placing your awareness in this area, your energy perception will open up to new possibilities for healing. If you are deciding to move to a certain town, you can visualize the new town and your energy perception will explore the possibilities that the new town can offer you.

After you have focused on your question until it is very clear, and visualized your image, let it go and let your thoughts relax. Focus on your personal rhythm—your heartbeat or your breathing. Note any thoughts that come into your mind, even if they don't seem to make sense. You can always ask further questions, such as what a specific feeling represents or why a certain image appeared at this time. Also pay attention to your feelings. The Universal Wisdom accessed through the Vortex is multidimensional and experienced through our perceptions.

When you feel finished, bring your awareness back to the Vortex. Visualize the diamond getting smaller, take it back between your hands, and bring your hands back in front of your Vibrational Light Center to close off the Vortex. Sit for a minute in the other Vortex and allow your thoughts to get clear. Then close off the second diamond Vortex the same way. Have a notebook and pencil waiting. You may want to write down your thoughts, feelings and impressions from this exercise. We receive information in many dimensions within the Vortex and sometimes it is difficult for our brains to translate everything. Information obtained in the Vortex is like a dream; it can lose a lot in translation and will fade quickly. Keep your notebook in a convenient place so you can come back to your notes later and remember more of the details to answer your question. As you re-read your notes, you will gain a deeper understanding.

It is helpful to spend some quiet time after you do the Vortex Meditation and also pay attention to your dreams that night because Universal Wisdom triggers thoughts in your mind that will continue working long after you close off the diamond Vortex. More information may come into your awareness or your answer may become clearer after a few hours. You may also choose to return to the Vortex again to ask your question for more information.

Exercise 9: Energizing Your Vortex Energy Centers

Now that you have aligned your Truth Lines with the Vertical Vortex, and your Memory Lines with the Energy Band, you can use the Vortex to energize your Vortex Energy Centers.

We have Energy Centers, or Energy Vortexes, that are located at the places in our body where energy is exchanged between our Energy Web and our physical body. Each Vortex Energy Center is connected to one of the organs that govern our primary body functions. Energy flows through these centers horizontally, front to back. As upright creatures, we are constantly moving through the concentric energy circles that extend out into the atmosphere from the matrix of Mother Earth's Energy Web. When our Energy Vortexes are open, the energy from Mother Earth's concentric circles flows through us as we walk. When we blend our Energy Web with Mother Earth's Energy Web, we experience a peaceful state of being.

To begin, prepare the Vortex the same way that you created the diamond Vortex in the previous exercises. Each time you create a Vortex, start with all of your finger joints touching and then separate your hands to create the Energy Band. Work with the Energy Band, and then bring your hands back together, connecting your fingers joint to joint. Open your hands again and allow the energy to line up between your hands to form the diamond Vortex. Wait until you feel the energy of the diamond become strong between your hands.

Move both hands together at the same time to maintain the integrity of the diamond. Gently place the Vortex directly over the Vortex Energy Center by putting one hand in front of the Vortex Energy Center and one hand behind it. Hold the diamond Vortex between your hands while you energize each center. You may feel different energy at each Vortex Energy Center. Do not put an intention into the Vortex. Simply allow the Vortex to do what is needed at each Vortex Energy Center. When you are finished with each Vortex, bring your hands back together to close off the diamond. Create a new Vortex for each of the Vortex Energy Centers.

Your Vortex Energy Centers are the places where energy is exchanged between your Energy Web and Mother Earth's Energy Web, and your Energy Web and physical body. Placing the Vortex on your Vortex Energy Centers harmonizes the Energy Centers with your personal vibration, removes energy blocks, and increases the energy flow throughout your physical body and Energy Web. Energizing your Vortex Energy Centers brings a peaceful state of being, physical and emotional health, and the ability to adapt with the Earth Changes.

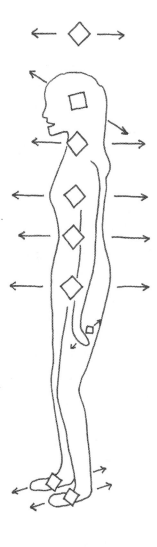

1. Center of Universal Awareness

In Your Energy Web directly above the top of your head) One hand in front, one behind.

2. Thought Center

Front of forehead to base of skull in back of head.

3. Sensory Centers

In front of both eyes to back of head.

4. Throat Center

Front of throat to back of neck.

5. Heart Center

Center of breastbone to mid-back, between the shoulder blades.

6. Center of Being

One hand right above navel, the other on the back directly behind it.

7. Reproductive Center

One hand above the pubic bone, the other hand on the sacrum.

8. Center of Creativity

On the palms of each hand. Energize with both hands together.

9. Grounding Centers

On the sole of each foot. One hand in front of the toes, and the other hand behind the heel. Do each foot separately.

Exercise 10: Fine Line Meditation

Humans are both physical and energy beings and we interact with the world energetically through our Fine Lines. Your Fine Lines are energy strands that extend out from your Vortex Energy Centers and connect with people, situations, animals and locations in the environment. When you meet someone, the first thing you do is extend one of your Fine Lines to make a connection. This is an unconscious process that enables your Energy Web to touch the vibration of that person and establish a sense of comfort. The feeling of instant attraction, like you have known this person all your life, is an interpretation of the vibrational energy encountered by your Fine Lines. In this case, your fine lines are letting you know that this person's energy has a similar vibration as yours. A feeling of unease or caution is another message felt through your Fine Line encounter that lets you know the vibration of this person or situation is incompatible with yours.

When we choose people as friends, part of the bonding process involves making a Fine Line connection with their Energy Web. When we have sexual relationships, particularly strong Fine Line connections are made between the Energy Webs of both persons. Once these Fine Line connections are made, we continue to carry them within our Energy Web. This can be a wonderful thing if the connection allows us to share deeper levels within a trusted relationship. The energy shared through that kind of Fine Line connection energizes and replenishes us. However, if the relationship changes or ends, or if we move from a situation or location, we may continue to carry the Fine Lines that are connected to them. These old Fine Line connections can drain our energy, cause emotional and physical discomfort or pain, and hold us back from personal growth. It is helpful to periodically clear the unnecessary Fine Line connections from your Energy Web.

This exercise is a meditation that will enable you to visit your Vortex Energy Centers and dissolve any Fine Line connections that you no longer need. I like to visualize the Fine Lines as electrical appliance cords plugged into my Vortex Energy Centers. Some of these Fine Line cords are ones that you have sent out and some are Fine Line cords that others have plugged into your Energy Web. Some of the cords are very small and delicate. Only a small amount of energy is shared through these cords. Other cords are larger and have different purposes. A few cords are huge and plugged in very tight. These cords can either share large amounts of replenishing energy that inspires and motivates you, or they can drain large amounts of energy and cause you to be sluggish, unfocused, depressed or sick.

When you visualize your Vortex Energy Centers, you will look with your inner eyes and see the Fine Line cords that are attached there. Go slow and take the time to feel the energy of each one of those cords. Is the cord small or larger? Does it have a significant color or feeling that can tell you something about the energy? Does this cord make you feel good? Is this cord a necessary connection that you have chosen? Is the cord one that does not feel comfortable? Is this cord draining you? Do you wish to keep this energy connection? Is it time to let this energy connection go?

It is not important to name the Fine Line cords. For example, you do not have to recognize that a particular cord is attached to a certain person, location or event. It is not even desirable to know where the Fine Line cords have originated, for having that picture in your mind will keep you in an emotional state and distract you from perceiving the energy attached to the cord. Keep your perception within your Energy Web. Assess each cord through the energy you feel from it. Then, choose to keep the connection or let it go. For those cords you want to release, visualize yourself gently pulling the plug of the Fine Line cord out of the receptacle of your Vortex Energy Center. Unplug the cord with gratitude, and watch it slowly shrivel up and fade away now that you are no longer feeding it with your energy.

You can do this exercise by yourself as a meditation, or you can share this exercise as a meditation to guide another person to clear out unnecessary Fine Line attachments. Begin by finding a quiet space where you will be undisturbed. You can be sitting or lying down. Allow yourself to get very relaxed by taking at least five slow, deep breaths. Keep your thoughts in the present moment. Breathe into your physical body and feel yourself relax even more when you exhale. If you are tense in any area, let your breath flow into and around that area and carry the tense energy away. Allow your body to spread all the way out to its edges; and let each part of your body float in its place supported by the energy of your breath.

Breathe next into your Energy Web. Let your breath flow around and through this energy field that surrounds your physical body. If you encounter heavy or blocked energy, let your breath flow through the energy block and gently dissolve it. Allow your Energy Web to flow all the way out to its edges, and feel yourself supported by the Universal Energy Web like a cloud floating in the sky. Let your breath energize and sparkle your Energy Web.

In this exercise, you will take your awareness into each of your Vortex Energy Centers and visualize the Fine Line connections that are attached at these centers. The process is the same at each Vortex Energy Center. Allow yourself plenty of time to perceive each Vortex Energy Center. Notice what it feels like in this energy center. What does it look like? How is the energy flowing? Are there any Fine Line cords connected there? Considering them one at a time, notice what the Fine Line looks like: its size, shape, color, how it makes you feel, and if it belongs there or needs to be unplugged. If there is a Fine Line that needs to be released, gently unplug the cord, thank this energy, and watch it shrivel away. If there is more than one Fine Line that needs to be unplugged, release them one at a time. Notice how different your energy is now that you have released the Fine Line(s).

Follow this sequence to visit your Vortex Energy Centers and visualize your Fine Lines.

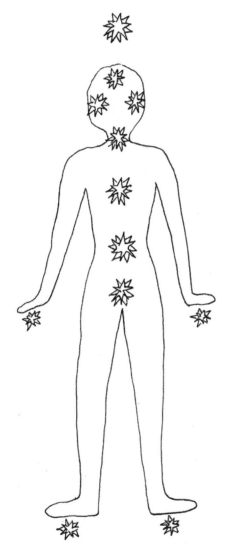

1. **Center of Universal Awareness**- Accesses Universal Wisdom. *(In your Energy Web above your head)*

2. **Thought Center**- Conscious awareness and intuition. *(In your mind behind your forehead)*

3. **Sensory Centers**- Perception using all senses. *(Behind your eyes in the center of your head)*

4. **Throat Center**- Communication. *(In your throat)*

5. **Heart Center**- Balance and relationships. *(In your heart, center of chest)*

6. **Center of Being**- Vibrational Light center, Spirit Essence. *(Right above your navel)*

7. **Reproductive Center**- Self Image. *(In your sexual organs, womb or testicles)*

It is also possible to include these Vortex Energy Centers.

8. **Creative Centers in both hands**- Manifestation. *(Palms of both hands)*

9. **Grounding Centers in both feet**- Earth Connection. *(Soles of both feet, at the instep)*

When you have finished this meditation, bring your awareness back to your breathing. End with a Vertical Vortex or balance your Truth Lines. If you are working with someone else, working on either the Truth Lines or Vortex Energy Centers is a nice completion. Do not do too much Vortex Energy work after clearing the Fine Lines, as this is a big energy shift for one session.

Exercise 11: Star Energy Vortex

Now that we have entered the Fifth World, our energy flows directly out from our Center of Being—where our Vibrational Light Center and Spirit Essence are located—in the pattern of a star. After many years of working with the Vortex in the previous exercises, I was told that the Fifth World energy had now solidified and we should work with the Vortex on our star energy flow pattern. I like to do this Vortex exercise in the morning, as it is both expansive and energizing. When the star energy gets flowing, it opens the door for making connections and manifesting.

Prepare by doing an Energy Band. When you are finished, bring your hands back together and open up a Vortex. Wait until you can strongly feel the energy of the diamond line up between your hands. Now, spread your hands wider apart and place them on either side of your waist while visualizing the diamond Vortex resting within your Vibrational Light Center. In this exercise, you are going to visualize energy flowing out from your Vibrational Light Center in the pattern of a star. By visualizing these energy pathways, you set your energy in motion for expansion and luminescence. While it is possible to direct the energy flow in this Vortex, we do so without intention, simply visualizing our energy flowing and shining.

Leave the energy pathways open and flowing when you close off this Vortex. You can later share your star energy by sparkling your eyes at everyone you meet. Your star energy will automatically touch another person's star energy and they will get energized through sharing your energy vibration. People often respond with a noticeably positive reaction.

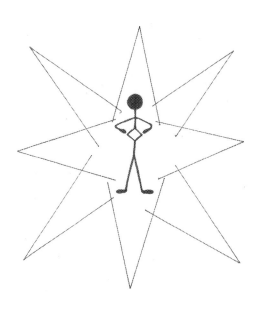

1. Visualize your energy flowing from your Vibrational Light Center down into the Earth.

2. Visualize your energy flowing from your Vibrational Light Center out into the Universe.

3. Visualize your energy flowing from your Vibrational Light Center directly out in front of you to connect with the Web of Life.

4. Visualize your energy flowing from your Vibrational Light Center directly out behind you to connect with the Web of Life.

5. Visualize your energy flowing from your Vibrational Light Center up past your left shoulder and out into the Universe.

6. Visualize your energy flowing from your Vibrational Light Center down past your right hip and into the Earth.

7. Visualize your energy flowing from your Vibrational Light Center and up past your right shoulder and out into the Universe.

8. Visualize your energy flowing from your Vibrational Light Center and down past your left hip and into the Earth.

9. Visualize these energy pathways in all directions flowing strongly, pulsing with your vibration, and full of shining light to share.

Vortex Healing With Others

When we are in the Vortex, we are in Sacred Space, directly connecting to the Vibrational Light Center of the Earth and the Vibrational Light Center of the Universal Mind. When we work with another person in the Vortex, we share their Sacred Space. Following the teachings of the Medicine Wheel, we are mindful to approach Sacred Space with honor and an attitude of Unconditional Love. As love expands into appreciation and gratitude, we open the door to healing and growth. This is the thought foundation upon which the Vortex operates. We create the most effective Vortex when our feelings are aligned with these principles.

Within the Vortex, both the giver and receiver expand into multiple dimensions. However, there is no danger of being overwhelmed with energy while using the Vortex. When the doorway to the Void is opened, everyone can take whatever they need. Our Guardian Spirit works with us in the Vortex to assure that we take only what we need for positive growth at the present time. The effects of the Vortex can be intense. Physical manifestation happens as each person is ready to accept those changes. Energy moves very fast in the process of rearranging and transforming. It is possible to release years of trauma or pain. It is common for pain to be relieved through one or several Vortex sessions because as our vibration shifts, so does our awareness and physical structure. On a very unconscious level, we each decide how much transformation we are willing to receive and it is there for us.

Specific changes cannot be pushed however. Many times the healing that occurs happens exactly where it is needed, though not where we might expect. Reflection or meditation can reveal these subtle transformations. It is always advisable for both the Vortex giver and receiver to rest for a time after a Vortex session to allow the energy to complete its process of rearranging. Often the results of a Vortex session are noticed much later, after a good night's sleep. The Vortex always brings a more balanced, relaxed state of being.

Vortex energy works with transmutation. Therefore, both the person creating the Vortex and the person receiving the Vortex enter the Sacred Space of the diamond. Since both have the opportunity to access from the Void, both experience the gifts of the Vortex. Because both people are simultaneously in the Vortex, there is no chance of picking up someone's negative energy. All energy is brought into perfect alignment with each person's individual Truth.

I always feel energized after I do a Vortex session. I like to follow the advice that I give the person I am working on—take some time for yourself to let the energy become fully integrated within your physical body and Energy Web. I also drink lots of water to facilitate the energy flow. I once worked on a Reiki master who asked the secret of why I didn't get drained from working with energy. It's simple: Always put yourself in the Vortex first, and then create another Vortex to work with the other person. When we put ourselves in the Vortex first, and then open a Vortex to work with others, it increases the flow of harmonizing energy. Everyone benefits.

Before you work with someone, find a quiet place where that person can be comfortable. You can choose to work on the floor or on a massage table. The person can be sitting or lying down. Whatever you choose, make sure that you can comfortably work without physical strain and distractions.

Especially if you have had a hectic day, you may need to spend time by yourself centering and grounding before you are ready to open the Vortex. Always choose to reschedule the Vortex session if you are unable to get centered. Chaos can result if your energy is unstable when you open the Vortex. Approach the Vortex healing session with thoughts of gratitude for the potential that is always available for us. Keep your mind clear with thoughts on sharing loving energy. Listen to the guiding voices of your Spirit Guides as you work, they will call your attention to what needs to be done.

Begin at your Vibrational Light Center with your right hand over your left hand. Slowly unfold your hands and bring your palms together with the joints of your fingers touching. Allow both sides of your body to balance rhythms, and then take five slow deep breaths. Get centered. Fully experience your wholeness. Pull your hands apart, create your Energy Band, and go through the entire process of aligning your energy just as you usually do with the Energy Band. This can be done prior to the session in a separate place, or you can do your Energy Band while the person is relaxing before you begin to work.

When you finish with the Energy Band, bring your hands back up in front of your Vibrational Light Center. Focus your attention on the space between your palms and feel the energy line up to form the Vortex. Let the Vortex image become strong and clear, then visualize the Vortex diamond becoming large enough to place your entire physical body and Energy Web inside. Move your hands close to your body so that you are standing inside the doorway of the diamond Vortex. Keep your thoughts clear and focused on Unconditional Love. If any other thoughts come into your mind, allow them to be released, without emotion, into the Vortex. Do not close off this Vortex. Visualize the diamond anchored in place around you when you bring your hands back together. Open your hands again, create another Vortex, and place the person inside. Leave both Vortexes open for the entire healing session. At the end of your session, always remember to close each Vortex while standing in the same location and position as you were when you opened it.

It is important to allow the person time to reorient after the Vortex session. We need to adapt to the transforming energy and physical changes before going on with the days activities. I usually leave the room for about fifteen minutes to allow personal time and then return with a drink of juice, herb tea, or flower remedies and maybe some crackers. Conversation also helps with the transition from the Vortex session into ordinary life. While we are snacking, I pass along information that I perceived during the session and respond to any questions or concerns.

Valuable feedback is often related after Vortex sessions. Since you are working directly with that person's Sacred Space they may feel vulnerable, so this time is important in developing trust. Don't hesitate to share vague or seemingly unrelated thoughts. Sometimes I receive clear images while working in the Vortex and, even though they mean nothing to me, I always find that they are significant for the person I am working with. After a brief conversation, the person is usually ready to safely drive home. I always suggest scheduling a few unstructured hours after the Vortex session so that the person can continue integrating Vortex energy without feeling responsible for daily activities right away.

If you forget to close off the whole body Vortex for yourself or the other person, you or the other person may feel disoriented after the session. If that happens, take a moment as soon as you remember to center yourself, breathe, and visualize yourself back at the time and location where the session ended. Visualize yourself returning to the position where you originally opened up the Vortex, gently take off the diamond Vortex, visualize it shrinking until it is back between your hands, and then close it off. Remember to center yourself with a Vertical Vortex afterwards. Because the Vortex works outside of time, this is effective even if you are no longer in physical proximity with the person.

In the following exercises, you will open one or multiple Vortexes while working with another person. If you have trouble keeping the Vortex image clear, close off that Vortex and start again. When you put yourself in the Vortex, you automatically transmute any energy you don't need through the Vortex doorway, so you can access the Vortex energy of transformation within yourself. As you create possibilities for another person, you create possibilities for your own energy changes. We are all tightly woven together in this Web of Life and Vortex Energy opens the pathways of sharing our energy connection in a very nourishing way.

Remember, the Vortex is always opened without intention, so the healing energy you share has unlimited possibilities. (Remember the story of Sue?). The Star People tell us that the process of creating the Vortex must be followed as given, however feel free to experiment with the structure of the session to find what is best suited for your needs. You need not include all of these exercises in one healing session. Indeed, it would overwhelm the person with too many vibrational shifts at the same time. Use your intuition to determine where the energy needs to shift and when that process is complete.

During your initial whole body Vortex, closely perceive the person's energy to understand what is needed at this time and then follow your feelings. Any single exercise or combination of exercises would be appropriate. A good first session might include aligning the Truth Lines and Memory Lines. If the person needs balancing and healing in specific areas of their body or for emotional issues, you might want to work with the Vortex Energy Centers and Memory Lines. Once you start working with an exercise, for example energizing the Vortex Energy Centers, you need to finish it or the person will feel out of balance.

I do not recommend combining the Vortex with other methods of energy work, simply because the Vortex does quite a bit of shifting and rearranging energy and it is preferable not to overload the person in one session. However, I have used the Vortex with massage sessions and found that it extends the healing of the massage by working on both the physical body and Energy Web. This is simply done by putting myself and the other person into the Vortex, leaving it open, and then giving the massage. If necessary, I will open another Vortex on an area that needs releasing and then continue the massage. The Vortex can also be opened prior to receiving any kind of healing work or medical treatment.

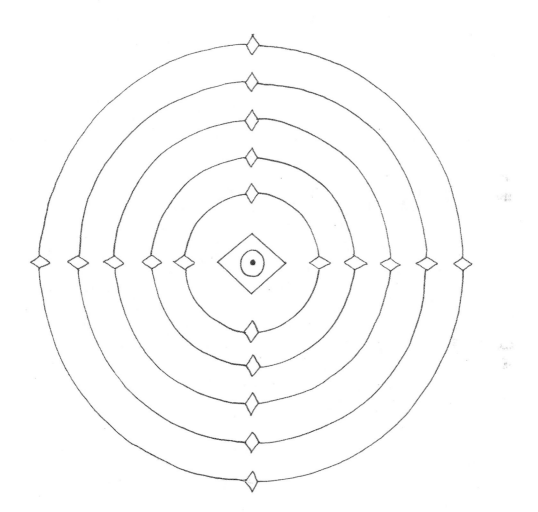

Exercise 12: Truth Line Alignment For Another Person

Make a comfortable place for the person to lie down during this session. Before you begin, take five deep breaths and put yourself in a Vortex. Leave the Vortex diamond open around yourself, make another diamond Vortex, and place it around the person. Leave this Vortex open while you bring your hands back together and make an Energy Band. Once the Energy Band is open, move your hands apart so the Energy Band is stretched long enough to work along the Truth Lines in the steps below. (This is similar to the sequence that you used to align your own Truth Lines with the Vertical Vortex, however you will be using the Energy Band to align another person's Truth Lines.) Leave the Energy Band open at each Truth Line long enough to feel the energy shift and flow between your hands. Then gently take the Energy Band back into your hands, bring your hands back together, and make another Energy Band to align the next Truth Line.

When we align the Truth Lines, we open up the energy pathways that flow through us between the Earth and the Universe. It is important not to cross the Universal Wisdom Pathway when aligning the Truth Lines. Therefore, stand on the left side of the body when you work on the left Truth Lines, and stand on the right side of the body when you work on the right Truth Lines. You can align the Truth Lines on the front of the body while the person is lying on their back and then ask them to turn over so you can repeat the process on the back of the body. Make sure that the person is comfortable after the position change. Repeat the steps on the back of the body, making sure you start on the left side and work toward the right side. When you have finished aligning all the Truth Lines, you can choose to end the Vortex session by first closing off the Vortex that you left open around the person, and then closing off the Vortex that you left open around yourself. Or you can choose to continue the Vortex session by aligning the Memory Lines as described in the next exercise.

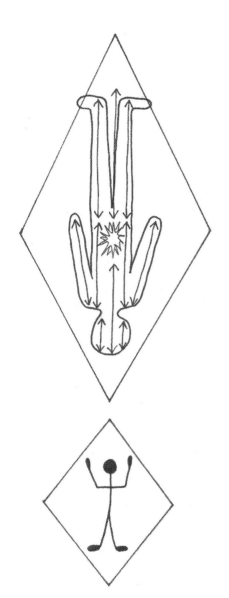

1. Make a Personal Vortex around yourself, leave open.

2. Make a Whole Body Vortex around the person, leave open. (For the Following Positions, Make an The Energy Band to Use on The Person's Truth Lines)

3. Left shoulder to palm of left hand.

4. Left shoulder to top of head, left side.

5. Left shoulder to left hip.

6. Left hip to bottom of left foot.

7. Left shoulder to bottom of left foot.
   Place the Energy Band at the person's center and expand both hands in opposite directions so they extend from the top of the head to below the feet.

8. Right shoulder to top of head, right side.

9. Right shoulder to right hip.

10. Right hip to bottom of right foot.

11. Right shoulder to bottom of right foot.

12. Right shoulder to right palm.

13. Close off both diamond Vortexes if the session is finished.

Exercise 13: Memory Line Alignment For Another Person

You can align another person's Memory Lines after you have done a Truth Line Alignment or other Vortex work. The person should already be lying down and comfortable. This Memory Line Alignment is similar to the way that you aligned your own Memory Lines. It is important to open the Energy Band in the center of each Memory Line Cross and then extend your hands to the correct position for each step. When you are finished with each step, it is important to close the Energy Band in the center of the Memory Line Cross. Otherwise, you will scramble the electromagnetic energy charge on the side of the body that you reach across. Begin standing at the head of the person. As you work down, you will need to move to the side. It does not matter which side you chose to stand on. Just be sure that your left hand continues to work on the left side of the person and your right hand on the right side.

I use the Memory Line Alignment at the end of a Vortex session for grounding, as it brings the person's energy back into their center. You can spend a few minutes with your left hand on the left foot and your right hand on the right foot when you reach the end of the Memory Lines, and then slowly move your hands out into the Energy Web before disconnecting. When you finish this alignment, remember to close off the Vortex that you had opened around the person at the beginning of the session and also the Vortex you left open around yourself. If you chose to continue working with the Vortex during this session, there is no need to open additional Vortexes, just leave these open and begin the new exercise.

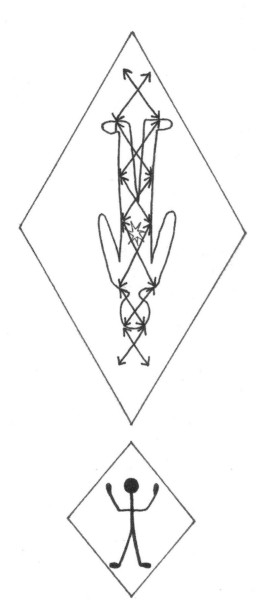

1. Make a Personal Vortex around yourself, leave open.

2. Make a Whole Body Vortex on the person, leave open.

3. <u>Memory Line Cross in the Energy Web Above Head</u>:

> Right Hand in Energy Web, Left Hand on left top of head.

> Left Hand in Energy Web, Right Hand on right top of head.

4. <u>Memory Line Cross at the Sensory Center</u> (In front of nose):

> Right Hand on right top of head, Left Hand on left shoulder.

> Left Hand on left top of head, Right Hand on right shoulder.

5. <u>Memory Line Cross at the Heart Center</u>:

> Right Hand on right shoulder, Left Hand on left hip.

> Left Hand on left shoulder, Right Hand on right hip.

6. <u>Memory Line Cross at the Reproductive Center</u>:

> Right Hand on right hip, Left Hand on left knee.

> Left Hand on left hip, Right Hand on right knee.

7. <u>Memory Line Cross at the Calves</u>:

> Right Hand on right knee, Left Hand on left foot.

> Left Hand on left knee, Right Hand on right foot.

8. <u>Memory Line Cross at the Feet</u>:

> Right Hand on right foot, Left Hand extended below left foot in Energy Web

> Left Hand on left foot, Right Hand extended below right foot in Energy Web.

9. Close off both diamond Vortexes if the session is finished.

Exercise 14: Vortex Healing

This Vortex sequence allows us to help another person adjust their energy vibrations. As the evolutionary changes are now in full swing, a Vortex healing session can bring both yourself and the other person into balance simply by allowing energy to rearrange and adapt to the new vibrations. Within the diamond Vortex, we have the opportunity to manifest balance in our lives by energizing our personal vibration. It's best to approach this session with no expectations, and trust that you both will receive what you need. We never use personal intentions when we do the Vortex for another person, as we cannot assume that we know what's best for them at any given time.

Begin by creating the diamond Vortex and put yourself inside. Leave this Vortex open around yourself when you bring your hands back together. Take five deep breaths and make another Vortex. When you feel the diamond energy get strong, pull your hands apart and visualize the Vortex getting large enough to completely surround the person that you are working with. Place this diamond Vortex around the person and leave it open throughout the entire session.

Bring your hands back together and follow the sequence below. You will be creating Vortexes within the original Vortex that you placed around the person. At each Vortex Energy Center, create the diamond Vortex between your hands. Gently place the Vortex into the Vortex Energy Center. (Place your hands on either side of the head while visualizing the Vortex surrounding the Thought Center, for example.) While in the Vortex, your hands may remain still or begin to move on their own. Let your hands work without thinking about what you are doing. You are rearranging energy and will intuitively know what is needed. You will sense when its time to move on.

Close off each Vortex before going on to the next Vortex Energy Center. Start the process of creating the Vortex over again at each Vortex Energy Center by creating the Energy Band and then allowing the Vortex diamond to form. Be sure to use the Vortex at all the Energy Centers in the steps below so the person is balanced at the end of the session. There are many additional Vortex Energy Centers in our physical body and Energy Web. Most are located at the joints or within the organs. If you sense that any of these Vortex Energy Centers need work, create a Vortex and work on that Energy Center in a similar way. You can also place a Vortex on any area that is holding pain.

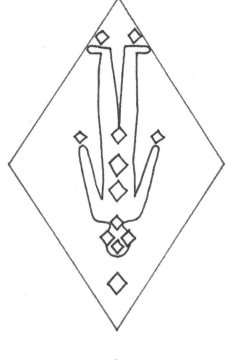

1. Make a Personal Vortex, leave open.

2. Make a Whole Body Vortex on the Person, leave open.

3. Make a Vortex on the Center of Universal Awareness.

4. Make a Vortex on the Thought Center.

5. Make a Vortex on the Sensory Centers.

6. Make a Vortex on the Throat Center.

7. Make a Vortex on the Heart Center.

8. Make a Vortex on each of the Creative Centers.

9. Make a Vortex on the Center of Being.

10. Make a Vortex on the Reproductive Center.

11. Make a Vortex on each of the Grounding Centers.

12. Close off whole body Vortex on the person.

13. Close off your personal Vortex.

Exercise 15: Heart Vortex

The Heart Vortex can be done with two or more people. This is a real nice way to share energy with others. In the process of making this Vortex, you extend Unconditional Love from your Heart Center to share with another person. The more love we give away, the more love is available to circle the Earth, and even more love returns to each of us. One of the first steps in evolving into the Unity of Oneness is to share Energy Webs. I believe that if we all shared our Energy Webs frequently, we would create such an uplifting vibration around the planet that social inequality and wars could not be supported. Begin by sharing the Heart Vortex with your family and friends. Sharing Unconditional Love enhances intimate relationships and healing on all levels. It is also a positive way to deal with conflicts and disagreements.

The process of creating the Heart Vortex is the same whether there are two people or a group. Sit or stand facing each other or facing the center of the circle. Make sure to maintain eye contact with all of the others during the time you are creating the Heart Vortex. It is advisable to select a facilitator who can move the group through the steps.

Take five slow, deep breaths to center your energy. If you have any concerns or discomforts, allow them to be released at this point. Keep your thoughts in the present moment. Breathe deeply, transmuting any limitations into pure light. When you are ready, do a Vertical Vortex. Follow all the steps of the Vertical Vortex, and then bring your hands down to rest at your sides. You will not use your hands to create the Heart Vortex.

When the group is ready, have everyone bring their attention into the Heart Center. Feel the love and peace that you hold in your heart. Gather all the love that you have to share. Then, extend that love out to merge with the love of the others in the center of the circle (or merge in the space between two people). When all the love merges in the center of the circle, the diamond Vortex is formed. This diamond is exactly the same as the one that you created between your hands, only now it has the magnified energy of all participants. In this case, you have created the diamond Vortex through extending your love and you can use this Vortex to manifest love in the world. You might perceive the love in the center of the circle as a light or shimmering energy. Hold that image strong and clear.

While we are in the Heart Vortex, everyone should think only of Unconditional Love. After a while, the Energy Webs of all participants will reach a similar vibratory frequency. When that happens, everyone can place a healing color in the center of the Vortex to make a rainbow, or everyone can together chant a healing sound into the Vortex. You can visualize the Earth, or a particular place or person, inside this Vortex. Anything that is placed inside the Vortex will be surrounded by Unconditional Love. As always, we will not use an intention in the Vortex, we will simply share love.

Stay in the Heart Vortex as long as it feels comfortable. Then visualize the diamond Vortex being released. Each person will slowly take their energy back. All of the love that was in the Vortex now returns to the hearts of the participants. It is common to feel energized after the Heart Vortex because each individual's love has multiplied. Hugging is appropriate after closing the Heart Vortex, as hugging is a physical way of sharing love energy. Another way to share Energy Webs is to place your right hand (the give-away hand) over your heart for a moment, and then extend this hand to the heart of another person to share your love. Working with the Heart Vortex brings us into the unity of One Heart.

Exercise 16: Group Vortex

The Vortex recreates One Mind. When we merge our energies together in the Vortex, we accelerate the evolution of the Universal Energy Web. The vibration created by a Group Vortex sends out a call for everyone, everywhere, to remember our common connection through the Web of Life. The Group Vortex is a wonderful way to share energy with others physically present in the circle and also those who are unable to be present.

Before doing a Group Vortex, the group needs to choose a focus for the Vortex energy. For example: the Group Vortex could be done for a person in need of healing; to send Vortex energy to someone far away; to encompass a specific situation so that it will manifest the best energy and opportunity for all involved; to encompass world events or political leaders so that they take right action for the best common good; to encompass the Earth or specific locations or species to foster balance and survival.

Remember, we are simply placing the person, species, events, or Earth into the Vortex without intention or attachment to a specific outcome. When we place someone or something into the Vortex, all of the energy needed for the right course of action will become available. It is not up to us to judge what the right course of action will be because we are not able to see the total Universal Plan. We simply open the doorway of the Vortex and focus on the image without any intention.

It is advisable to select someone to talk the group through this Vortex so that everyone works together. Start with everyone sitting or standing in a circle. Each person should balance the energy on both sides of their body by putting their hands together and allowing their energy to come into a harmonious flow. When each person feels balanced, they should place both hands on their Center of Being (Vibrational Light Center). The right hand should be covering the left hand with thumbs touching and pointing upwards. Take five slow deep breaths together.

Next, have everyone unfold their hands, bring their palms and the joints of their fingers together, and create the diamond Vortex. Energize the Vortex by visualizing the energy inside the diamond clear and sparkling. When the image is strong, everyone will turn their hands into the center of the circle at the same time, merging the individual diamond Vortexes into one large Group Vortex. Have the group energize this Vortex. Next, everyone should visualize the chosen image inside the Vortex diamond. Visualize the person, event, or place surrounded by Vortex energy. See the visualization as shining energy receiving the transformative gift of Vortex energy. Hold this image for a comfortable period of time. If it feels appropriate, everyone can place a healing color in the center of the Vortex to create a rainbow, or everyone can chant a healing sound together while in the Group Vortex. The leader should be aware of the group energy so that the Vortex ends before people start losing their concentration.

When you are finished, have everyone gently release the visualization from the Vortex. Allow the colors to remain as a Rainbow inside the diamond. If you have placed sound in the Vortex, allow the vibration from the chant to remain and merge with Universal Harmony. Instruct everyone to take their personal diamond Vortex, and some of the Rainbow, or Universal Harmony, back between their hands. At this time, it is possible to ask each person to enlarge their personal Vortex so that they can sit inside the Vortex for a while. When each person finishes, they should close off the Vortex by bringing their hands back together, joints touching.

After closing off the Group Vortex, place your hands on the Earth (or visualize your energy extending down into the Earth through the floor) to energize the heartbeat of Mother Earth. Then, hold your hands up to the sky, (or visualize your energy extending up into the sky through the ceiling) to energize Father Sky. Bring your hands back to your Center of Being and draw the energy, Universal Harmony and Rainbow into your Vibrational Light Center. Complete the exercise by making a Vertical Vortex.

Exercise 17: Using the Arc

Definition of an Arc:

"A band of sparks or iridescent light between two closely placed electrodes when the current leaps the gap from one to the other." (Electricity)

"The curved path of a star or planet sphere." (Astronomy)

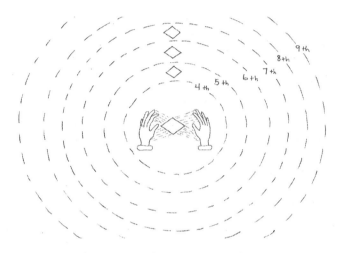

The Vortex Is The Doorway To The Arcs

We already know that when we place our hands in the position to create the Energy Band and leave our hands in this position for awhile, the energy molecules polarize—magnetically attract—to form a focal point which becomes a diamond shaped energy Vortex. The energy molecules that form the diamond are drawn very closely together within the magnetic energy beam created with our hands. This dense energy creates an intense vibration that opens the door to the Void—the place of all possibility. The Vortex diamond has the ability of a laser to rearrange energy, working directly through your Vibrational Light Center to affect the vibratory resonance of the structural building blocks of your energetic, emotional, cognitive, and physical bodies. When you work with another person in the Vortex, they are similarly affected by the ability of the Vortex to rearrange energy. Since the Universal Energy Web connects all beings through their Vibrational Light Centers, each Vortex has a shifting effect on the entire Web of Life.

As the energy molecules between your hands magnetically attract to form the diamond Vortex, the surrounding energy molecules are pushed away. These energy molecules form the shape of a sphere around the diamond Vortex and your hands. The energy molecules in the sphere are widely scattered and form a light, yet very sensitive layer of energy. This is the Arc. The Arc is a more expanded dimension of energy awareness, including a deeper energy perception, a more expanded consciousness, and a deeper understanding of Universal Laws.

There is an infinite number of Arcs surrounding each Vortex, like ripples that form on a pond after you throw a stone into its depths. Starting with the Vortex between your hands as the center, as you move outward, the energy molecules move further and further apart. The Vortex is the doorway into the Arc. You can only go so far in the Arc until your reach another Vortex that is the doorway into the next Arc. Each Arc enters a higher dimension with more expanded energy. No space, time, or physical locations exist in the Arcs. The Arcs expand indefinitely to the limits of the Universe.

When we create the Vortex between our hands, we are also opening the doorway to the Arcs and the Void. It is possible to enter the Arcs and connect with the wisdom of the Universal Mind. In the Arcs, just as in the Vortex, we observe energy with our multidimensional sense of energy perception. We can ask questions, receive answers, and know what is about to happen following the current energy flow patterns. In the Arcs, we hear the Truth that is the rhythm of the Universe. It takes patience and thoughtful meditation when working with the Arcs, because the messages and insights that we receive are not easily translated by our physical perceptions and language.

It is best to proceed slowly when working with the Arcs. When you enter the Arcs, your awareness and energy expand as the energy molecules scatter. Each time you go into the Arcs to access information, you experience increased vibrational energy. Remember, you will return with a lighter density than when you started the Vortex session and these energy changes will manifest on the physical dimension within your emotions and physical body.

I worked with the Vortex for about three years before the Star People gave me the information on the Arcs. I suggest that you work with the Vortex awhile and feel confident with your perception of energy before exploring the Arcs. Experience has brought to my attention the need to remain grounded and proceed slowly in the Arcs. Otherwise, your vibration may have difficulty shifting as you travel through dimensions and you may return disorientated. Again, please keep your thoughts clear and focused on Unconditional Love. While in the Vortex, and especially in the Arcs, thoughts that arbitrarily come into your mind can easily manifest. Now that we have entered the Fifth World, manifestation is immediate. We are the creators and our thoughts are our reality.

I use the Arcs to access information for others and myself. As previously stated, we cannot assume that our physical perception can reveal the correct location or extent of energy imbalances. However, if we enter the Arcs with a clear mind, we will be able to ask questions and perceive the Energy Web with our multidimensional perception, thus discovering a true picture of how energy is flowing. Often, I am surprised at what is revealed in the Arcs that I did not consider. Additionally, working with the Arcs allows us to work on many physical and energetic levels. We can move within time, space and location, enabling us to go back to the exact time and place of an injury and then create a Vortex from that perspective; we can do precise work with someone who is far away; or we can work inside the body in very small places, even within the DNA of our cells.

There are multidimensional Beings in the Arcs that can guide us, teach us how to work with multidimensional energy, and help adjust energy vibrations. I have learned many things from these teachers and guides. My advice if you encounter one of the multidimensional beings is to go slow and listen within. There are those out there who do not have our best interest in mind and those whose vibrations are much more expanded than ours. Spending too much time with either of these types of beings can get very disorienting. For these reasons, I stay in the first three Arcs and always close off the Arcs and the Vortex if something doesn't feel right or if I feel my energy getting drained.

Entering the Arcs

You can use the Arc while doing a Vortex Healing session. If you are not already working inside a diamond Vortex, begin by taking all the necessary steps to create the Vortex. Work slowly and clearly. Stay aware of your energy at each step. Balance the energy on both sides of your body; make and use the Energy Band to polarize your energy; and then create the diamond Vortex between your hands. Place yourself inside the Vortex. If you are working with another person, make a second Vortex and place that person inside this Vortex. Stay inside the Vortex awhile and allow your energy to rearrange. Then, slowly allow your thought awareness to go through the Vortex doorway and enter the Arc. You will feel the spaciousness and expansiveness of the Arc, a much different energy than the diamond Vortex. Allow yourself a few moments to adapt to the vibration of the Arc.

The first Arc is the Fourth Dimension, the dimension where our Energy Webs exist. In this Arc closest to our physical and emotional bodies, we can best access information for bringing physical and emotional situations into balance. Once you are comfortable within this Arc—and in an open, receptive state—you can ask a question. If you don't reach this state for the first few times, don't worry, just continue to get used to the vibration of the Arc and wait until you feel comfortable. You may perceive colors, shapes, shadows or sounds. Ask what these mean and listen for an answer. If you don't understand something, ask for clarification. Sometimes in the Arc, I observe where energy is stuck or out of balance; other times I am given colors in the Arc that I can use with the Vortex to expand the healing. Once you develop your multidimensional perception, you will be able to work on many levels using the Vortex and the Arc.

Inside this Arc is another Vortex diamond that is a doorway into the next Arc. If you go through this doorway, you will be in the Fifth Dimension. When you go through the Vortex in that Arc into the next Arc, you will be in the Sixth Dimension and so on. There is an infinite number of Arcs and each one expands our awareness into a new dimension. As you go further from the physical dimension, the less you will be able to translate the experience back into the thoughts and words of our Third and Fourth Dimensional reality.

Use caution when entering the more expanded dimensions. When we use the Arcs, we transmute the Earth as well as ourselves. Energy changes, often very subtle, occur within the surrounding environment, the person we are working on and ourselves. We access Universal Wisdom, bringing in the knowledge to make good choices based on Universal Truth. We are here on the Earth at this time to help shift the vibration of the planet into harmony with Universal Wisdom and Truth. If we shift our dimension too much, or too quickly, our vibration will become out of balance with the planetary energy. Our eagerness can unintentionally create chaos within many dimensions. It is in our best interest to stay grounded and connected to the Earth.

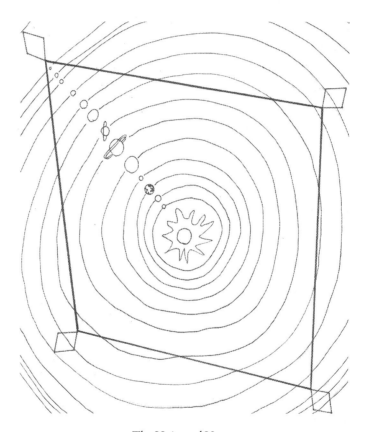

The Universal Vortex

Universal Vortex

We can travel through the Arcs while doing personal Vortex work, in healing or group work, while sitting on the Earth in an Earth Vortex, or at the location of a natural Vortex on the planet. The exercises in this book explain only a fraction of the potential found within the Vortexes and Arcs—those Vortexes that we can create through visualization or with our hands. Many other Vortexes exist naturally in space. These Vortexes can be larger than entire galaxies or so small that we cannot see them. Everyone is affected when we pass through these Vortexes whether or not we are attuned to the Vortex Energy.

Our solar system is continually moving through space. The planets rotate while they follow their individual orbits. Solar systems move together in a harmonious rhythm. The Universe pulses and evolves with each breath. Visualize the way we worked with the Arcs in the previous exercise, and you can understand the movement of planets and Vortexes in space. As she follows her orbit, the Earth occasionally passes through a Vortex—a place of intense, compressed energy vibrations within the Universe—and then moves into the Arc—a place of expansion and growth within the Universe. Sometime later, the Earth will pass through another Vortex and later still, another Arc. The solar system periodically passes through Vortexes and Arcs on its journey through space.

Just like the Vortexes that we can create, the Vortexes in the Universe exist outside of time, space and gravity. For the past twenty-five years, our solar system has been traveling through a Grand Universal Vortex. We entered this Vortex in 1988, passed through the Vortex Center in the year 2000, and left the Vortex in 2012. This is a rare occurrence, as the last time our solar system passed through the Grand Universal Vortex was about twenty six thousand years ago. The Mayans documented this transition through the progression of days in their calendar. Inside the Grand Universal Vortex is the pure vibrational field that is the Essence of Being. This is the place of the Universal Mind and the Universal Dream where we all originated. We can touch the Truth of existence within the Grand Universal Vortex because here we can access all the Fields of Knowledge. Understanding is perceived on many levels within the Vortex. Not limited by our senses, we encompass awareness, interact with geometric energy configurations, and resonate with Universal Wholeness. We absorb Universal Wisdom through every cell within our body and throughout our Energy Web.

The Vortex Energy within the Grand Universal Vortex has interacted with the Energy Webs of all life, triggering an awakening that is the foundation for the evolution of new species. As we passed through the Grand Universal Vortex, we reconnected with our Spiritual Home and received a renewed appreciation for the Wholeness of Life. Our conscious awareness now manifests our true place in the Universal Dream. Whether we are aware of it or not, this awakening has affected us on the physical, mental, energetic and spiritual levels of being.

Our consciousness is drastically changing and our vibration intensely altered as we evolve along with the Earth. In recent years, we have been physically adapting to changing universal vibrations, changing rhythms and cycles of the Earth, and changing personal rhythms. In order to survive and evolve, we each must connect with Mother Earth and all life. Together, we are One Planetary Energy Being sharing the same rhythm of life. Therefore, as the rhythm of life on planet Earth changes, we must adapt with her because we all must evolve together. If we hang on to the old vibration, we become separate from the process of planetary evolution and our existence cannot be supported.

Since we maintain rhythm through our breathing and heartbeat, many people have experienced illnesses as their breathing and heartbeat rhythms shift gears to adopt a new vibration. The changing vibrations may also make us feel sluggish, tired or unable to concentrate. We can develop headaches or stomachaches and experience trouble sleeping. If we let go of expectations and allow ourselves to flow with the new vibrations, our energy becomes lighter, we feel better, and life becomes easier. To maintain physical health during this time of vibrational shifting, it is essential for us to get enough rest, nourish ourselves with good unprocessed and uncontaminated food and water, accept our physical abilities without pushing ourselves past our limits, let go of emotionally toxic relationships and situations, and take the time to sit on the Earth and become a part of the natural world.

The geometric energy configurations within the Grand Universal Vortex have triggered an awakening of our latent DNA. The timing of this passage through the Great Universal Vortex resonated with the coding deep within our cells and called them to respond to a dimensional energy leap. Our physical body is now restructuring on the cellular level. Latent abilities, character traits and physical adaptations are starting to develop. As we evolve into a new species, humans will fully become the manifestation of the Universal Dream of Wholeness. The DNA awakening is further explained in Part Five: Tidbits of Universal Wisdom, Sacred Geometry and DNA.

The multidimensional Fields of Knowledge within the Grand Universal Vortex have transmitted vibrations, feelings and images into our conscious and unconscious awareness. Every person has the Wisdom of the Universe available to her or him now—no wonder we feel like we are on mental overload sometimes! Life may appear confusing, as relationships and situations are changing so quickly that we aren't able to deal with it all, and we are confronted daily with many choices that we don't have enough information about to understand. We may go through memory lapses and periods of confusion as our brains adapt to the increased vibration and multidimensional awareness that we don't yet have a frame of reference for understanding.

Because Universal Wisdom is accessed through the Fields of Knowledge, we are ready to create the reality that we choose. Since we have everything available to us, we each must decide what we want to manifest. When we focus our thoughts and ask our questions, we are able to learn much more than ever before. Once we can perceive the multidimensional Universal Wisdom, we will be able to find the answers to all of our questions and create solutions to solve our challenges and problems. It is not a difficult task to learn this skill. What is necessary is to open our minds, sharpen our inner perception, and trust that everything we envision will manifest at the right time. This is a big responsibility, for whatever we manifest affects all life.

The energy of the Grand Universal Vortex is changing and transforming our life. At times, it may seem like things are out of our control and we are just an observer along for the ride. Then at other times, the situations that resonate with our thoughts and energy vibration will effortlessly materialize, people that have similar attitudes and goals will suddenly appear, and things that we have envisioned will manifest immediately. Situations that are not supportive to our personal vibration will collapse. As a result, emotions may become volatile. We may go through periods where we feel disconnected and overwhelmed; while at other times we fall into place with the new vibration and put together our best creative work and intellectual breakthroughs.

To maintain our perspective during this time of shifting vibration, we must learn how to clear our minds from mental chatter so that we can ask questions and then listen within for the answers. It is no longer necessary to rely on others to tell you what to do. Since we can each access Universal Wisdom, we are each wise enough to make our own right choices. Trust that what you need to know will guide you to become the very best that you can be.

Our emotions are going through a process of transmutation triggered by the Grand Universal Vortex. We already know that we store thoughts and emotions in our Energy Web, and after we carry the same thoughts and emotions around for an extended period of time, they move into our physical body to be stored in our cells. The thoughts and emotions of our parents and grandparents are passed on to us through our physical inheritance of DNA and these are also stored in our cells.

The Grand Universal Vortex has triggered the releasing of these old emotions from our physical body and Energy Web. This means we may feel like we are riding an emotional roller coaster at times as the thoughts and emotions that we were carrying for so long come out and demand attention, seemingly at the smallest trigger. We may not even know what it is that we are clearing out, but the process continues without our conscious knowledge or approval. In fact, we are processing for the entire history of our human Ancestors. When you find yourself in this situation, know that you are experiencing a normal part of evolution. It is essential to let go of all old emotions now. It's best to allow quiet time when you are clearing so that your vibrations do not affect others. At least walk away for a few minutes to center with your heart-beat and breathing rhythms before communication with others. Fault and blame do not have a place here. Understand that these feelings are not within your Spirit Essence, they are just a part of your earthly experience. Don't dwell on them, instead give over to the flow with com-passion, as we are all releasing together. Always keep your thoughts focused on positive images. Honor your Spirit Essence for choosing to live at this time. Be grateful. Allow Unconditional Love to teach you how to nourish yourself and each other.

Planetary and personal changes intensify when we move from a Vortex into the Arc. All life on Earth had been feeling the vibrational effects of the Grand Universal Vortex for almost a hun-dred years before we entered it and we will be adjusting to the new vibrations and multidimension-al awareness for many years to come. As we move into the Arc, these Earth changes will intensify. The Earth is also evolving physically, energetically and spiritually. Storms and natural occurrences such as earthquakes are changing the physical landscape of the planet. The energy of the Universal Vortex has brought a new rhythm for the planet, as we now experience the seasons with unvcharac-teristic weather patterns and fluctuating temperatures. The cycles of life have changed with the new vibration and this is reflected in the cycles of growth and reproduction of all species. Every being on the planet is experiencing the energy changes of this Universal Arc as we realize our potential and align with the Universal Wisdom of Truth. Spiritually, Mother Earth's dream is the same as ours: to become One Planetary Being with the Awareness of Wholeness.

The Grand Universal Vortex has called us to come home. We are connecting as One Planetary Energy Being living with a common awareness. This is the culmination of our spiritual journey; becoming whole with all that exists. Our entire view of living is changing, as we become part of the Wholeness of Being. Through connecting with all life we do not lose ourselves, but instead expand ourselves and increase our vibrational light energy. We bring our awakened awareness of wholeness into our relationships and situations of living through the feelings of love and compassion. We embrace All Our Relations and live with their welfare in mind. This is the first step in our energy evolution that will eventually help the planet evolve into One Energy/light Being in the Seventh World.

Vortex Transformation

A glow like fire, laser light energy
Pours out between my fingers,
Connecting the threads of my being
In an intricately woven Energy Web.
The glow sounds a resonance
Which lines up the very essence
Of all the tiny particles that are my being,
Shifting them into new patterns.
Energy flows, DNA is triggered,
Life is renewed, regenerated, reprogrammed.
The light glow awakens a new rhythm
Allowing us to adapt to the New World.
Underneath the beauty, pain and love,
Each one of us is light energy experiencing life
On a mission to explore all being
In all places in this vast Universe.
My intricately woven Energy Web
Is connected to a larger Energy Web
Which connects to all Energy Webs of all beings,
Of all worlds in all dimensions of the Universe.
Light energy = Life manifesting thought dreams.
Like tiny sparks our thoughts ignite energy.
The world takes on a new form to meet our expectations.
We are Sacred Creators, weavers of light energy.
Light energy heals, transforms and changes
The rainbows flowing within and around.
The essence of Pure Love is the purpose of being.
There is no separation—we were always only One Essence of Universal Life.
Awaken and know the gift you share.
Feel the light energy burn within your hands.
Bring in the fire of pure intention.
Sparkle your eyes and watch your light shine,
Reflecting the Universe within your soul.

The Vortex Doorway: Into The Arcs

Exercise 18: The Vortex Ladder

We know that we are a part of the Universal Dream of the Great Mystery, and connected in the Grand Energy Web. Each of us was envisioned within the dream, and then following Universal Timing, each Spirit Essence came into a physical body to live out our purpose. During the birth process, a Spirit Essence enters a physical body by traveling on energy strands that are woven together to look like a row of Vortex diamonds stacked on top of each other, reaching out into infinity. I call this the Vortex Ladder because it looks like a ladder to the Spirit World. This pattern of diamonds linked together is the energy pathway through which our Spirit Essence enters the Earth Walk at birth and returns to the Spirit World at death.

The Spirit Essence anchors in its physical body while it is still inside the womb of its mother (or inside the egg or seed). The energy that the Spirit Essence brings, which includes the coding for what that Spirit Essence will manifest during its physical life, swirls around its Vibrational Light Center and forms the Energy Web that will surround this physical body for as long as the Spirit Essence lives within it. The first thing to manifest is a physical structure that carries the coding, or blueprint, for the physical body. When the Energy Web merges with the physical form, the coding takes on the physical form of the Vortex Ladder, the double helix of our DNA. We carry this Vortex Ladder within the core of each cell in our body. Our DNA coding continually manifests our physical characteristics. Some of our DNA coding remains dormant until triggered. Some of the DNA coding can change as our physical body and Energy Web change. The DNA coding of our Vortex Ladder follows Universal Timing and ensures that we manifest our part in the Universal Dream.

The Vortex Ladder opens automatically when a Spirit Essence comes into the Earth Walk. I saw this Vortex Ladder when my daughter was born. During the birth process, the Vortex Ladder helps to integrate the Spirit Essence with the vibration of the physical world, easing the shock of entry.

The Vortex Ladder makes an Earth Connection for the Spirit Essence and begins the exchange of energy between the Spirit Essence and the physical world. When the Spirit Essence comes into the Earth Walk, it anchors energy cords at special locations on the planet through the Vortex Ladder. These locations carry energy vibrations that are most similar to the energy vibration of that Spirit Essence. We carry our connections to these special Earth locations in our Energy Web for as long as we live, and thus we are intimately tied with the energy at those locations. That means we are always sharing energy with these special Earth locations; whatever our vibration is at any given time is also shared with that location, and the events at that location affect our energy vibration. When Earth changes or human intervention occurs at our special location, we will feel it in our Vibrational Light Center. When we send Unconditional Love and healing energy to our special location, the plants and creatures living there feel it. In this way, we are each a part of the living Earth and the Earth is a reflection of All of Us.

It is possible to open up a Vortex Ladder when a Spirit Essence is about to leave the Earth Walk at the end of life. Simply go through the steps to balance your energy and then open the Vortex. Visualize the diamond strong and clear. Allow the diamond Vortex to expand in a pathway, extending out into the Universe. You will see this as the diamond replicating itself over and over, stretching into infinity throughout the Universe. What you are actually seeing is the pattern of Vortex doorways that sit at the entrance to the Arcs. Let the Vortex Ladder become a strong image, then place your hands, along with the Vortex Ladder, over the person. (Or visualize this process if you are not in the same location as the person.) Since the Vortex Ladder is the most basic image that our Spirit Essence knows, the person will remember the path leading back to the Spirit World. I have assisted many people and animals with the Vortex Ladder to make a comfortable passage. Leave the Vortex Ladder open around the person. Take it off after the Spirit Essence has left the physical body or, as it happens in some cases, the person makes a recovery. It is not necessary to be physically present when opening up or closing the Vortex ladder.

The exercises using the Memory Lines and Vertical Vortex connect us with the Vortex Ladder and reestablish our connection with our personal special locations on the Earth.

Time Vortex

Situations and events exist only for a specific duration of time. However, situations and events occur within many dimensions of our awareness, and often simultaneously. The idea of time passage developed within our conscious awareness as a means of keeping events separated so that we could most fully experience each individual occurrence. Within the Fourth World of separation, time evolved into a separate entity that has come to dictate a rhythm of living. Fourth World time exists outside of our awareness, moving us to act out scenarios of separation. This way of looking at time, represented by our watches, is not a part of Universal Truth.

Time in its purest form transcends dimensions. It is unlimited and fluid—affected by the relationships and perceptions of the participants within situations and events. Since the foundation of time is within our awareness, time changes as our perception changes. This Fifth World way of perceiving time honors personal rhythm through the process of creation, growth and change.

The Universe is based on timing (as opposed to time). Everything happens at exactly the right moment of readiness. Timing allows the Universal Dream to unfold with its perfect rhythm, within all forms in every dimension. When we plant seeds and watch them sprout, when a mother bird sits on an egg, when a fetus develops within the womb, when animals begin to hibernate or migrate, when flowers bloom and when the leaves on the trees start to turn colors, we witness natural timing.

To understand timing, we must forget the clocks and allow natural rhythms to move our personal cycles of living. Observe the rising sun, the subtle changes that move the day along, and the gradual change from sunset into night. Notice the very small everyday changes as the seasons blend into each other. Watch the animals—they are great teachers of natural rhythms. Certain events, such as astrological occurrences, follow larger cycles of timing. As each cycle of timing moves, it brings small or major changes to the energy vibrations surrounding the planet.

There are Vortexes and Arcs within timing as found in the natural rhythms of the Universe and we can use them to move through time. For example, if a person has had an injury, you can open up a Vortex and go into the first Arc to travel back to the location and time when the injury occurred. It is not necessary for you both to have been present at the physical location and time of the injury. Just have the person visualize the exact time, place and emotions that were experienced at the point of injury. You can then connect with that picture to move both your energy body and the person's energy body back to that time point. You do this by opening the Vortex, moving into the first Arc, and intending to go back to the time point. It is not necessary that you see this image clearly; you will know you are there when you feel the energy shift. If it is too emotional for the person to remember, just focus on the time and location and have the person relax.

After you are in the visualized time point, open another Vortex to work with the person at the physical site of injury. (Open a Vortex and place it on their leg if they broke their leg in an accident, for example.) While you work, have the person visualize a rainbow, or chant a healing sound, to help them let go of the situation. When we work with the Vortex this way, changes occur retroactively from the time point of the injury. It is difficult to explain how this can occur, but remember time is cyclical. This is the most common way that I work with time points in Vortex healing. Timework is best done in the first or second Arc because these Arcs are the energy doorways closest to the physical dimension.

Vortexes of different durations exist in time, some of them longer than many days and some of them only seconds long. We experience smaller Vortexes in time when events seem to slow down so that many things happen in what we perceive a very short period of time, or we experience one of those days where we accomplish very little as time seems to speed by. It is also possible to physically step into Time Vortexes and step out into the past or future, but that is beyond our human capabilities at this time. As we work with the Vortex, we will learn more about time and our place within the natural rhythms of life. As dimensions shift, we will be able to transverse longer time spans and distances in the Vortex. When we develop our latent DNA, we will exist outside of time and perceive the reality of Wholeness.

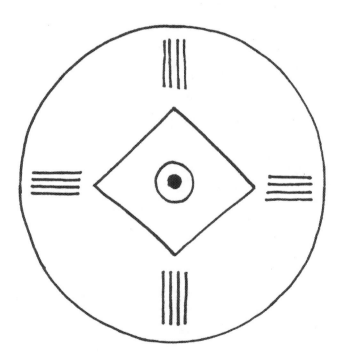

THREE INTERPERTATIONS OF THE VORTEX SYMBOL

COSMIC

Universal Mind, Universal Vibrational Light Center.

Universal Dream-Envisioning energy & life within the harmonious quality of the circle. Circular planets assume circular rotations. Cycles and seasons begin.

Doorway from the Void to Creation of form. Transformation & manifestation.

Energy expands in all directions and dimensions. Life experiences from every perspective. The Dream unfolds.

Universal Dream completed. All Worlds return to the wholeness of the Universal Energy Web, the ONENESS from where we all began.

PHYSICAL

Seed of being (Envisioned within the Universal Dream). DNA coding.

Personal dream for living. Your purpose & commitment. All potential for growth. We choose the situations of our Earth Walk.

Doorway of the womb. DNA manifests your physical form of being.

Growth & learning in 4 stages: Learning, growing, seeking & sharing wisdom. The four navigational directions & the four elements.

Completion of your life cycle. Fulfillment of your personal dream through your contribution to the world.

SPIRITUAL

Self-awareness, Spirit Essence, Personal Vibrational Light Center

Personal Medicine Wheel reveals the qualities & gifts we choose for this Earth Walk. Personality manifests.

Energy Web that surrounds physical form. Boundary of your personal Sacred Space.

Energy expanding, connects us to Web of Life. Motivation to carry out your purpose for living.

Personal wholeness realized. Fulfillment of your purpose & commitment. Personal energy vibration becomes a permanent part of the Web of Life.

PART FIVE: TIDBITS OF UNIVERSAL WISDOM

The energetic matrix of our Universe is geometric forms. Within the smallest atom you will find geometric patterns, and behind the atom, within its Energy Web, you will find the geometric patterns of movement that manifested its physical form. Geometric forms hold the wisdom of our past, present and future. Learning to use geometric forms to align our personal energy will unlock our full potential as creators.

Using Colors

Do you ever wonder why you love certain colors? Everyone is attuned to colors. Each of us comes into this Earth Walk with personal colors that carry our vibrational light and represent our creative gifts. We carry colors in our Energy Web as a reminder of the Great Mystery's dream of living. Each color and shade carries a specific vibration that can trigger healing responses. All of the colors together create a rainbow that carries the vibration of Wholeness.

The wonderful thing about using colors for healing is that you can simply bring a color into your thoughts, wear a color, or use colored lights to allow this energy to work. You do not have to consciously manipulate or direct colors. Colors work on everyone in an individual way, so we are all positively affected by the colors around us. Many schools of thought assign meanings to colors, but I prefer to work with colors on a vibrational level, using intuition as a guide for what is needed for any one person at any given time.

The Star People have given me a way to use colors with the Vortex. Whether working on myself or another person, the process is the same. First, I complete the entire Vortex session up to the point where I am ready to close off the whole body Vortex around the other person (and myself). At this point, I return my hands to the Energy Band position in front of my Vibrational Light Center, about 8-10 inches apart. I visualize the diamond Vortex between my hands. Then, I go out into the first Arc, reach my hands up to the Universe, and ask the Multidimensional Beings for a healing color.

I usually perceive the color as a ball or sphere of colored light between my hands. Very slowly, I take the sphere of color and move it down to my head, going from the left to the right side, sort of painting my Energy Web and physical body with the color. I make sure that I place the color on each one of my Vortex Energy Centers and on my Universal Wisdom Pathway, Truth Lines and Memory Lines. Sometimes I stay a few moments in certain places and let the vibration of the color interact with my Energy Web. I continue this process until I have reached a place below my feet, and then gently disconnect the sphere of color from my Energy Web. Finally, lifting my hands back up to the Universe, I return the sphere of color with gratitude. If I am working on another person, I receive the color, begin at the place above their head on the left side, and going from left to right, proceed down the entire length of the body until I reach the area below the feet, disconnecting in the same way.

I have seen that, in the Third World, there were places of healing where colors and sounds were used for many purposes to restore health and attune vibrational light energy. In these huge halls, people did not walk, but rather glided on energy. Their perception was very different than ours, enabling them to work in many dimensions. The colors were kept in a very special place and skilled practitioners used them for individual healing, spiritual growth and planetary attunement. The sounds were similarly used. Both the color and sound healers were highly respected. The people there did not experience illness or discomforts, as the colors and sounds kept their vibrations in harmony with the Universal Energy Web. I believe that we can remember these talents that our Ancient Ancestors used with color healing and that we can use them with the Vortex work to bring harmony back to the Web of Life.

The following are the meanings of the colors as revealed to me during Vortex Energy work with the color spheres:

PURPLE- Awakens memories of our past lives to heal trauma from the distant past that has been carried over into present day relationships.

ROSE- Regenerates energy flow after shock or injury. A particularly good color for healing trauma. Brings stamina and strength to deal with prolonged stress. Helps open our mind to new possibilities.

PINK- Calms the emotions and restores inner peace. Centers and focuses awareness. Heals the effects of emotional overload and stress.

RED- Balances male and female energy within our Vibrational Light Center. Heals imbalances related to menstrual cycles and sexual energy.

BLUE- Restores physical health and heightens the perception of all the senses. Replenishes and renews all the body's systems: nervous, circulatory, skeletal, muscles, lymph, breathing, thought process and all brain functions, and functioning of all the organs. Awakens the intuitive ability to see with the eyes behind our eyes and hear with the ears behind our ears. Promotes intuitive perception in all dimensions.

GOLD- Gold symbolizes the pure essence of being that we call Love. Balances thoughts with emotions. Brings Unconditional Love, compassion, inner peace and self-confidence. Helps us understand our individual role in the total picture of the Universal Dream.

CRYSTAL- Balances our Energy Web through reconnection to the Web of Life and Universal Energy Web. Allows the gently release of unwanted energy, particularly Fine Line connections that are draining. Reweaves personal energy pathways within our physical body and Energy Web.

WHITE- The color of Vortex Energy. Balances our electromagnetic energy and attunes our energy vibration to align with our personal Truth. Polarizes energy. Sends our vibration out to attract what we need. Transmutes dis-ease into ease-of-being in harmony. Integrates personal and planetary energy through healing situations caused by the Fourth World of separation and control.

GREEN- Motivates vibrational triggers for growth. Integrates external stimuli and personal growth processes. Aids digestion. Nourishes the connection between body, mind and spirit. Helps us adjust to new situations and major changes. Grounds us and strengthens our Earth Connection.

SILVER- Represents Universal Wisdom. Aligns us with our personal commitment for living. Allows us to perceive Wholeness—seeing from all points of view—and thus make wise decisions. Fosters compassion for all other life. Increases our luminosity.

INDIGO- Anchors the Fifth World vibration of Wholeness. Indigo opens our awareness to the concept of We instead of I. Enables us to create new paradigms and role models for living cooperatively with a common mindset. Indigo Children are born with the gifts of this color and can teach us how to flow with the quickening pace of the Earth Changes.

Using Numbers

Universal Wisdom and Universal Law are encoded in the numbers we use. In the time of our very ancient Ancestors, knowledge of the symbols and numbers were kept by the Wise Ones and interpreted for the people through teachings and ceremonies. Now that we are in the Fifth World, each person has the ability to access the messages of the numbers in a more expanded way than just through counting. The meanings of the numbers, like the symbols, are also triggers that unlock personal wisdom.

0

Zero is the Void. Here is the potential for all that can be. No physical forms exist in the Void, yet all possibilities are contained within it.

1

One is the point of conscious awareness. When each Spirit Essence enters its physical body there is a conscious awakening. At that time, a connection is made with the Great Mystery and the Web of Life. The number one is associated with the promise that we each make when we enter the Earth Walk.

2

Two is the duality found within all opposites in the natural world. In every situation, there is both a yes and a no. Male and female, physical and spiritual, light and dark are all examples of the many teachings of duality. One of these elements must always be balanced with the other in order for us to live in harmony and achieve wholeness. When we expand our awareness past the place of one, we look inside the mirror to see our opposite self, the duality within.

3

Three is a triad. Within every duality, an opportunity for growth is presented. This additional element brings motivation for change based on right choice. Right choice is not simply choosing good or evil, which are only reflections of each other. Right choice always honors All Our Relations through following Universal Law.

4

Four is stability and provides a foundation for growth. This is the doorway through which we walk to new beginnings. Each time we enter the doorway; we attract opportunities that expand our experience of living. Four brings our lessons and allows us to develop our talents.

5

Five is creativity and growth. We use our gift of creativity to visualize situations for comfortable living and manifest solutions to our challenges and lessons. The ability to visualize allows us to overcome our obstacles by accepting the abundance within the Void. We always have the ability to manifest our visions. Five brings harmony and unity.

6

Six is expansion. Now, our energy extends out into new directions to touch All Our Relations. We share our energy to create positive situations for others. Sharing our gifts and developing community relationships foster self-esteem. We walk our Earth Path through actions that will leave a positive memory of our contributions after we are gone.

7

Seven is the union of the Earth World and the Sky World. The elements of the dualities become integrated here. Seven is also the doorway between the Earth World and Spirit World, the Seven Stars through which all universal life passes. This number has been sacred since the time of our First Ancestors and is used in ceremonies to access Spirit messages. There are Seven Directions on the Medicine Wheel. Seven brings a connection with all life—past, present and future.

8

Eight is the Spirit World where our Spirit Teachers and Ancestors live. Through our gift of intuition, we can ask questions and listen for answers from our Guardian Spirit, Plant Teacher and the Ancestors. If we honor their guidance, they have much to teach.

9

Nine is release. This is the give-away that occurs at the end of a cycle of growth. When we have completed a lesson, we release it with gratitude so that another may have that experience of growth. Our give-away opens the door for new opportunities and growth.

10

Ten is new beginnings. This is the place of metamorphosis through which we emerge as a new form to begin another cycle of growth. This opportunity is a rebirth, a blending of physical development with an opening of spiritual vision and understanding. Ten opens up our multidimensional perception.

11

Eleven brings us back again to consciousness. In this expanded dimension, we become a part of the Universal Mind, where our Spirit Essence originated. Now we merge into One Mind. Eleven represents the doorway through which we will pass when our species evolves into its collective dream of Peace.

12

Twelve is the Universal Energy Web. This is the template that the Universal Mind created to connect all life. The Fine Lines of all individual Energy Webs go out through Grandmother Spider's Web of Life and can be utilized to bring about personal evolution and planetary transformation. The result of actualizing the Universal Energy Web is the evolution of multidimensional life forms.

13

Thirteen is the Great Mystery, the sacred number that is the origin of the rhythm of all life. This is the boundary surrounding all of creation and all possible paths of growth. Here we experience everything that is possible. Thirteen is Wholeness.

There are many ways that we can use numbers and symbols to help us remember Universal Wisdom and Universal Law. Whichever you choose will be the right way for what you need to know. The information presented here is by no means complete, for each person adds their own interpretation to create a system of wholeness. Colors, sounds, vibrations, movements, and Mother Earth's natural energy centers all carry encoded messages of Universal Wisdom that help with our understanding of the Universal Laws. Through observing and listening, we can remember the wisdom to guide us on our path to wholeness.

Universal Wisdom is remembered when we recognize the rhythm of the Universe inside our Vibrational Light center, see it reflected in each of Our Relations, and then honor how everyone fits together within the Web of Life. Universal Law is the application of Universal Wisdom to daily living, so that all of our thoughts and actions benefit All Our Relations and the evolution of life, not only on the Earth, but including the entire Universe.

Universal Wisdom and Universal Law provide a foundation for our existence. Truth is the ability to perceive one's self as a unique part of the wholeness of the Universal Dream and to take this self-image into consideration as the basis for every thought and action on our Earth Walk. All life carries a responsibility to perpetuate Universal Truth through thoughts, words and actions.

Using Geometric Forms

Geometric energy forms comprise the Matrix of the Universal Energy Field. The circle, triangle, square, diamond, spiral and other mathematical shapes brought the Universal Dream into form. They were the first thoughts manifested, and they became the energetic building blocks that provide the structure for all physical bodies. Sunbeams, moonbeams, energy flowing through the polarities of our body, and energy that we share with others all consist of strings of geometric forms which trigger our energy and awareness in a response that connects us to the world around us. Indeed, geometric forms carry the Universal Dream and weave the Web of Life.

Geometric symbols are encoded into our thought patterns while we are still inside our seed (before birth) to remind us of our personal part in the Dream of Living. These symbols, known to all ancient cultures as sacred, are triggers for remembering the Universal Laws that hold the dance of life together in a harmonious rhythm, and the Universal Wisdom that anchors our Truth within our Earth Walk. These symbols determine the details of our physical body and the major events that we will experience during our life.

As the matrix of our planet, the rocks and stones carry markings encoded with geometric shapes. Within these symbols, the stones hold the vibration of Mother Earth and the dream for this planet. Some geometric symbols can easily be seen on the surface of a stone while others emerge only when the stone is placed in water. I have included information about reading and working with the geometric symbols found on stones for those readers attracted to the energy of stones.

Some stones carry Vortex Energy and can be used in healing to help rearrange or transmute energy. Many different kinds of stones can be used to balance our Vortex Energy Centers and remove blocks from our Energy Web. Working with stones is beyond the scope of this book. If you wish to work with stones, I recommend that you hold the stone, listen to its vibration and allow your perception to show you how to use it. Although I love stones and often use them in healing work, I do not recommend using stones when doing the Energy Band or other Vortex exercises in the book, as the vibration of the stone will distract your focus from the Vortex. Further, the stone will enter the Vortex along with you, and its vibration will be transmuted. I only place stones in the Vortex when their energy needs to be changed, and always without intention.

The Dot—The Vibrational Light Center—Awareness

The dot represents our Point of Origin, the Universal Dream woven into the center of the Web of Life. Within the dot is our awareness of existence, our Sacred Point of View. It also symbolizes the Vibrational Light Center of each living being where our Spirit Essence resides, and where the cord that connects us to Grandmother Spider's Web of Life is anchored. The dot is the seed that we brought into the Earth Walk, and encompasses all of the gifts that make up who we are. The dot contains all potential for survival and growth. It is the Great Mystery, where we begin and end our journey.

Dots are often found as markings and carvings on stones, left as records by our Ancestors. Dots by themselves can represent the Great Mystery or an individual creature being. Dots in groups and rows signal a direction of movement that implies cooperation, and can record a specific event that happened in the past. A dot with a circle surrounding it can represent the Universal Dream or the sun, or it can symbolize the Medicine Wheel that provides the teachings for living in harmony.

Using the Dot

◊ Use the dot in meditation and energy work to bring your awareness back to your Vibrational Light Center. Focus on the seed of your being and bring all of the pathways of your Energy Web within to nourish your Spirit Essence. Remember the light of Great Mystery that you carry within your Vibrational Light Center and your commitment to the Universal Dream. Feel the unlimited healing and strength within your Vibrational Light Center. Notice the colors in your personal rainbow—and the sounds of your healing song—that you carry within your Vibrational Light Center and use the colors and sounds to help you remember your purpose for this Earth Walk. Always return to the dot, your Vibrational Light Center, before speaking or taking action.

The Circle—The Web of Life—Equality

The circle represents the Universal Dream and is the pattern of the Web of Life. Through its round shape, the circle manifests the Universal Law of Equality. All creature beings sit on the Medicine Wheel in an equal place, with no one ahead of or behind the others. Each one contributes their unique gifts to create the wholeness of the circle. The circle also symbolizes unity, for without the cooperation of each one of its members, the entire circle would fall apart. Our Energy Web is a circle, enclosing our personal dream for living, our purpose and contributions for the Earth Walk, and our personal Medicine Wheel.

The circle represents the female gifts of nurturing. The breast, the womb, and Mother Earth (the planet) are all circles. The circle is the doorway through which all life comes, and through which all life is fed. Mother Earth is represented by a circle to demonstrate her infinite life. She has always existed in the past, she is every expression of life around us at the present, and she will continue on indefinitely into the future. All cycles of growth and harvest follow a circular path, as do the rotations of the planets and stars in the Universe. The Universal Dream also follows a circular pattern—The Dream first envisioned and then manifested as life on all worlds of the Universe, life in the present being lived by all universal beings according to the Dream, and all life will eventually return to the Oneness of the Great Mystery.

The roundness of the circle establishes Sacred Space. Animals make their nests in a circle and our Ancestors made their camps in a circle. The Medicine Wheel is also a circle because it includes all of the teachings of Universal Wisdom and Universal Laws. We carry our personal Medicine Wheel in a circle around our Vibrational Light Center. The circle teaches us to establish and honor our own Sacred Space and reminds us to honor the Sacred Space of others.

Circles on rocks could signify Mother Earth, Grandfather Sun, Grandmother Moon, other planets, trees, clouds, or many other round objects. Circles could also represent family connections, community, clan and Sacred Space. Cycles of growth, such as harvest cycles and years of living, are also recorded as circles on rocks and in the circular growth rings of trees. Since the circle encompasses all of the Universal Wisdom, it can have many meanings. Use your intuition to remember the wisdom of the Universal Symbol of Life, the circle.

Use the circle in meditation and energy work to get to know your Sacred Space. Sacred Space includes all that you have manifested in this lifetime. Your physical body is your Sacred Space, along with your thoughts and ideas, feelings and emotions, and gifts and talents. By extension, your room, your home, your car and other possessions are also your Sacred Space. Honor your Sacred Space as the expression of who you are. Honor the Sacred Space of others as an acceptance of their contributions to the Web of Life. To honor the circle is to honor the Sacred Space of all beings. There is a lot to learn with the circle. Work slowly and take one step at a time.

Using the Circle

◊ Listen within to the rhythm of your physical body and learn the body's language so that you intuitively know what is needed to keep yourself healthy.

◊ Get comfortable, close your eyes and take five deep breaths. Open your perception to your Energy Web, and let your awareness go all the way out to the edges of your energy. Visualize your Energy Web as a sphere where your energy flows out only so far from your physical body before it returns to the center, your Vibrational light Center. Notice how your energy is flowing right now and where energy is blocked. Then let your energy flow through the blocks to release what is stuck there. Let the vibrational light of your energy shine brightly.

◊ Find the perimeter of your Energy Web. Visualize the circle as a sphere surrounding your physical body and Energy Web. You can work with colors in this circle to strengthen your Sacred Space and protect your energy from being drained. Simply select four to seven colors, blend them together into a rainbow and let that rainbow go out to become part of the circle surrounding your Sacred Space. You can also work with healing sounds to center your energy and harmonize your Sacred Space. Sing or hum your healing sounds or a tone that you feel is harmonious. Let the sound fill up the circle around your Sacred Space. Let the rainbow or healing sounds remain within your Energy Web and carry them as you go throughout the day.

◊ Sacred Space includes your thoughts, emotions, opinions and ideas. Visualize the sphere surrounding your thoughts and emotions when you need to keep centered.

◊ Place your hands together just like you do when making an Energy Band. Keep your fingertips touching while spreading your palms apart and you will form a sphere inside your hands. Visualize a person, a creature being, a situation, or a location on the Earth inside the sphere. Place your vibration inside the sphere and then surround your visualization with a rainbow or your healing sound. This is a great way to share your Sacred Space and send healing energy with others.

The Triangle—Manifestation

The triangle represents the Universal Law of Manifestation. Whenever a triangle appears, it indicates that there is an opportunity for a synthesis to occur between two opposing energies. The triangle's three sides create a space where we can connect a clear mental image with a strong heartfelt intention, and then bring these two together to create a new situation for positive growth. Manifestation occurs when all three of these elements are in alignment.

Triangles etched upon the surface of a stone can indicate a situation or conflict that has come into resolution. Encoded within each triangle is the solution to a dilemma or problem. In the Universal Language, triangles show direction and change. Triangular shaped stones were frequently used as trail markers by our Ancestors, and still can be found pointing a chosen direction in the locations where paths split.

Some stones have the shape of a triangle or pyramid where several triangles come together. This is especially true of quartz crystals. The top point of the triangle is a doorway. Our Ancestors have imprinted knowledge into the stones through these doorways. In a space of quiet meditation, go through the doorway and listen to hear their messages.

Using the Triangle

◊ You can create triangles to manifest changes in your physical body, Energy Web and relationships. During this process, you can use a clear intention for healing with a heartfelt feeling of acceptance to create a form for manifesting your vision. Sit in a cross-legged position with your spine erect and notice the triangle formed by your posture. The top of the triangle, your head, is the spiritual/thinking point. This is your perception—the Sacred Point of View that you bring to any situation. It also includes your gift of Universal Wisdom. The spiritual/thinking point provides motivation. Clarify your motivation and what you wish to manifest. Clearly visualize all the details of this manifestation. Accept it into your life.

The point on the bottom left of the triangle is the emotional point, encompassing feelings, relationships and expression. This point provides the connection. Look into your heart and be grateful for this manifestation. Make sure that you feel comfortable with all the details of this manifestation. Receive it into your heart.

The spiritual and emotional points form a portal through which we can create the physical manifestation. The bottom right point is the physical. Here we have the skills and talents, work and creativity to give form to our visions. The physical point provides the form for manifesting. Trust that what you need is waiting for you and it will appear when the timing is right. Work with your skills to fashion the vision. Hold your clear thought and grateful feeling throughout each step of the process. In this way, your creation will resonate with your vibration and bring joy into your life and the lives of others. Watch your creation manifest.

◊ It is possible to create triangles to align your Energy Web and stabilize your physical body. This is done by choosing points, usually within the organs and joints, and visualizing the triangular connection between them. See the appendix, Energy Alignment With Healing Triangles, for triangular placements.

The Square—Balance and Stability

The square symbolizes the Universal Law of Balance and Stability. The shape of the square represents the Four Directions on the Medicine Wheel that give us the teachings for living in harmony. Each direction brings in the opposite qualities than the one across from it, creating a balance with its opposing energy. Everything that exists is found within this balance of opposites. In our everyday life, we continually walk around the Medicine Wheel, learning and growing from the gifts of each one of the Four Directions. The four elements and four navigational directions are some other examples of the balance found within the connection between four qualities. The shape of the square reminds us to balance all that we have experienced and to avoid excessiveness with any one thing.

The square also represents the male gift of protection, teaching us to establish a boundary to define our Sacred Space. To live the Great Mystery's dream as a separate awareness, we need a boundary to maintain our individual identity within the Web of Life. We protect our boundary by honoring our gifts. When we understand that limitations are really gifts calling us back to our center—our Truth and Universal Wisdom—then we become stronger by sharing Great Mystery's light through our unique talents and gifts.

Very few stones are natural squares, although some stones contain squares within their markings. Squares etched on stones represent the Four Directions. To read the message within the stone, place the stone in your hand in the most comfortable position. If you were to draw a circle to represent the Medicine Wheel around the outer perimeter of the stone, in what direction does the square sit? The teachings of that direction hold important meaning for you. Look at where the lines of the square extend out to see the direction it is calling you to move into. What is this square telling you about your boundary? Reflect on your inner wisdom and notice where you can develop the qualities of this direction in your life.

Using the Square

◊ Visualize the square surrounding the circle of your Energy Web. Outside your Energy Web, your Sacred Space includes your room, your home, and your car—all that you own. Visualize balance and protection surrounding your physical Sacred Space in the shape of the square.

◊ When elements or relationships in your life become out of balance, meditate on the square to understand how to harmonize opposing energies. Get a piece of paper and draw yourself in the center of the square. Put yourself inside a circle to represent your Vibrational Light Center. Next, take a good look at what each direction (or side of the square) represents and label the four sides of the square accordingly. Look at the relationship of each side with its opposing energy on the opposite side of the square. From your position in the center of the square, figure out what qualities from each opposing side can be brought together to meet in the middle. Now you can redefine your relationship with the person or situation so that balance can be maintained. When you are sitting in the center of a circle or square, your energy is balanced and cannot be drained.

The Diamond—Vortex—Transformation

The diamond is the Vortex and the doorway to the Void. It represents the Universal Law of Transformation. As life continually recycles into new forms, the Vortex continually opens into the Void where the potential to meet every possible need exists. The Vortex is also a doorway to other dimensions and allows our energy to expand and transform as our species evolves to adapt to future circumstances and environments. The Vortex holds the key for integrating body, mind and spirit into Wholeness of Being.

Diamond shaped stones, and stones that carry the symbol of the diamond etched on their surface, carry the vibration of harmony for the Fifth World. These are healing stones. When placed upon your Vortex Energy Centers, or on parts of your body that are in need of healing, they open the doorway for energy to rearrange. For healing, use the stone without an intention. Be prepared to accept new possibilities as the harmony of Fifth Dimensional vibrations expands your potentials. Another use for a diamond shaped stone is to sit in a quiet place and go through the diamond doorway to meet the Spirit Teachers that speak through that stone. Ask your questions, listen for answers, and learn a new way for living. The shape of the diamond always calls us to change and transform in some way, so be prepared to enter the Fifth World as a new person.

Using the Diamond

◊ All of the Vortex Energy exercises in this book use diamond energy.

The Spiral—Great Mystery's Dream—Regeneration

The Universal Dance follows the shape of the spiral. All spirals reflect the movement of life as it was envisioned within the Great Mystery's dream for living. Spirals teach the Universal Law of Regeneration. Energy flows out from the center to be shared. At some point, the energy must return to replenish its source. There is a subtle balance in this dance that provides inner peace. Both giving away and receiving are necessary to achieve personal vitality. This is the foundation for comfort. Once we achieve a space of personal comfort, we can fully participate in the dance of the Web of Life.

The spiral is the symbol of Life Energy. The spiral reminds us to stay in the flow and to appreciate existence as a process. The Law of Regeneration teaches us that perfection is found in every moment, wherever we are, because we are exactly where we are supposed to be. Each moment is both the beginning and end of a process of growth.

Spirals were carved on stones by our Ancestors to remind us that we live within ever changing cycles. The spiral reminds us that, whatever the energy is now, it will eventually become the opposite. The secret of regenerating energy is our ability to move through the spiral and come out of it on the other side. When you find a stone with spiral markings, you are being called to surrender to the universal flow of life. The message is that new opportunities for personal expansion and growth are available for you to decide which direction to follow.

Visualize a double spiral comprised of both counterclockwise and clockwise turns. Moving out from the center, we find counterclockwise turns slowly increasing in size until the movement stops. The reverse movement starts almost immediately with clockwise turns moving in ever-smaller turns into a new center. The movement still does not rest, but continually repeats itself over and over. This is the energy pattern of life within the Universe. The Earth's rotation places our physical Earth Walk in a clockwise direction. This is the direction that we use to create. The hurricane and other destructive winds move in a counterclockwise direction, the direction of destruction or undoing. When we die and walk the Spirit Path, we will follow the counterclockwise energy direction. Understanding this will help you understand the symbolism of the Spiral Dance.

Using the Spiral

◊ Dance the double spiral when your energy needs regenerated or when you need to release. This dance is done outside. Find a place away from the path that you walk on everyday. Prepare to dance by envisioning the change it will bring. You will need an object symbolic of your release (what you are ready to give away) and a small seed (to symbolize what you are ready to accept).

First, hold a clear image of what you wish to release. Find something symbolic of the quality being released, or draw or write it on a very small piece of paper. Place your gratitude for this situation into the object and recognize the gift that also came with this situation. Make a small indentation in the Earth, place the symbol of your release inside and cover it up. Stand on that spot and begin a slow dance moving in counterclockwise circles. Breathe deeply and relax. Be grateful for those things that you have experienced and allow them to transform. Dance until you feel that the energy for releasing is complete.

Then, move to a new place a short distance away. Visualize what you wish to create (or the energy you wish to generate) that will take the place of the situation that you are releasing and place your vision into the seed. Allow that new image to come into your heart and accept it as manifested into your life. Make another indentation in the ground and plant the seed. Stand on top of this spot and begin the clockwise dance, slowly moving in clockwise circles until you feel that the energy for manifesting is complete. Plan to spend some quiet time after this dance appreciating your energy regeneration.

◊ The spiral can also be used to connect with someone or something. Visualize yourself as the center of the spiral with the energy spiraling clockwise around your Energy Web, then moving out and spiraling around the other person or thing. I use this spiral to connect with people who are far away, and also with special things that I send in the mail and my luggage at the airport. The spiral keeps the person or object connected with your Energy Web. My packages and luggage have always arrived safely at their destinations, and the people that I have kept within the spiral usually end up calling to say they are thinking about me.

◊ Use the double spiral when you have areas in your body that are inflamed or painful. Get into a comfortable position where you can be undisturbed. Take five very slow deep breaths and relax. Place your awareness into the problematic area and find the center from where the pain or inflammation is radiating. If your are experiencing emotional pain, go to the center of the painful feeling, the place that feels most uncomfortable. From within this center, visualize energy moving in a counterclockwise direction. Continue letting the energy spiral counterclockwise until you feel a shift in the energy or you feel that you have moved enough energy in this direction.

Continue visualizing the energy, and without breaking the energy flow, allow the counterclockwise energy to spin off to its side and start a clockwise energy spiral. Allow the energy to spiral clockwise for as long as it feels comfortable. You may get a feeling that the energy has shifted or that you are have completed the spiral. When you spiral energy in the counterclockwise direction, you set up the motion to dissolve pain or inflammation from your physical body and Energy Web. When you spiral energy in the clockwise direction, you set up the motion to balance and harmonize your physical body and Energy Web. Plan to rest, or be still for awhile, after doing the double spiral so that the energy can continue to shift. This is a good exercise to do before going to sleep as the spiraling energy continues to work after you fall asleep.

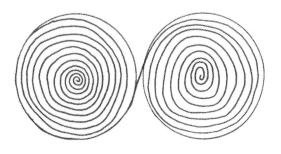

The Vortex is an open door.

Changes resonate through its Multidimensional Core.

Standing in Universal Truth, we open free

The channels to our Eternity.

Breathe deep and enter the place of Trust.

To release Limitation is our must.

When we enter the Diamond, our Wings unfurl

And we are transformed in its Central Whirl.

Expansion is evolving into the Unity of the Sun,

While in the Arcs, this process has begun.

As we open perception to the Universal Memory,

We can envision the Fifth World as it might be.

Love is the only Place to keep our Thoughts.

Peace is the only Action we have Sought.

When we stand in Trust, we are Ready to Change,

And inside the Vortex we will Rearrange.

Sacred Geometry and DNA

Sacred geometry holds everything in the Universe together. We call the geometric shapes sacred because without them there would be no life. The Universe is comprised of holographic geometric energy forms in numerical combinations: each one is an equation for manifesting energy into form. The Energy Web of every being is made up of holographic geometric forms constantly interacting with each other to create what we call reality. The holographic geometric forms are the building blocks that make up the underlying energy structure that determines what each physical body will look like. These holographic geometric forms are easily influenced by any other energy that they come into contact with, so they are always shifting and changing.

When the Shining Energy Beings that would become the planets, suns and stars emerged from the Great Mystery's dream of creation, they were simply masses of holographic geometric forms that moved out into the Universe. Each of these energy/holographic forms was programmed to follow a particular role within the Great Mystery's plan for the Universe and encoded with unique combinations of colors and sounds. As the masses of holographic geometric forms entered their rotations and slowed down their vibrations, they began to take on physical characteristics and achieve solid bodies in this physical dimension. It took many millions of years (as we know time) for the physical planet that we call Mother Earth to take shape. In fact, the world we live in today is but a momentary glimpse inside the evolutionary development of the holographic geometric forms that make up our planet Earth.

Every other being in the Universe has developed the same way. We each originated as a thought within Great Mystery's dream of creation, emerged from the dream as a Shining Energy Being, and then went out as a mass of holographic geometric forms to shape a physical body as it was developing inside our mother's womb. During this process, we made some major decisions about this lifetime based on our programming from the Great Mystery's dream. Choices such as gender, nationality and nation of birth were chosen before we entered the Earth Walk so that we could play our part in the evolution of the Universe. We also chose our parents, talents and special abilities, as well as major lessons and challenges that we would encounter so that we could learn and grow while we are here. Our physical bodies and many of the situations that we would encounter during our life are encoded in the holographic geometric forms that make the foundation for our personal Earth Walk.

We carry these holographic geometric forms within our Energy Web throughout our Earth Walk. We also carry colors and sounds that have special vibrations unique to our role in this Earth Walk. When we remember our geometric patterning, keep surrounded with our rainbow of colors, sing our healing sounds, and keep our thoughts and actions in harmony with the Great Mystery's dream, then our lives will be filled with Peace. Indeed, Sacred Geometry is the blueprint for maintaining balance in our personal life as well as the evolution of our species and planet.

Each creature that we see around us also has a foundation made of holographic geometric forms with a similar story of evolution. Even beings such as rocks are made of holographic geometric forms, and they change and evolve as their energy interacts with other energy. All beings are our Relations in the Web of Life, for we affect each other when our holographic geometric forms interact. Therefore all beings are all intricately tied together in an evolutionary process designed by the Great Mystery. There are also beings inhabiting all of the other planets, suns and stars in the Universe, and we are able to interact with many of them. Our Universal Relations may have physical bodies quite different than ours, or bodies of pure light, sound or energy. Our evolution is bound together as the story of the Universe, unfolding as holographic geometric forms create physical and energetic manifestations on many dimensions to experience living from every possible point of view. Understanding this relationship between all beings goes above and beyond our present scientific knowledge and calls us to remember the Universal Wisdom and Universal Laws.

The Universe communicates through geometric shapes. Unspoken intuitive communications travel in geometric form through energy vibrations, light, color and sound. These geometric shapes go out from a source to touch everything there is. Once the geometric shapes are formed, they keep traveling until they reach the very end of the Universe. Even if you do not see, hear or feel them, they can still touch every other being. The Great Law—or Universal Law of Relationships between all beings living in harmony within the Web of Life—is encoded within Sacred Geometry. Our present day language, mathematics, art and science are all based on Sacred Geometry.

Sacred Geometry carries the triggers for remembering Universal Wisdom. The holographic geometric shapes are encoded within the structure of our DNA. Originally humans were given a twelve-stranded DNA, and each DNA strand was encoded with a geometric shape to give us the gifts and abilities that we would need to survive here on this planet. We have lost the use of ten of those strands of DNA, or we may have been intentionally prevented from using these strands and accessing much of the Universal Wisdom that we need for our species' survival. Now that our planet has entered a New World, we are experiencing a shift within our holographic geometric forms and it is possible to regain the use of our dormant strands of DNA.

At this time, the Star People are returning to give us back the triggers. It is up to each one of us to Remember. When we do remember, the lost strands of DNA will begin to awaken and re-weave together. Right now we are experiencing an evolutionary shift into a new human species. The opportunity is here now for everyone's DNA to awaken and become whole once again.

Remember. Look to the symbols that the Ancient Ancestors of every land left carved on the rocks, painted on cave walls and woven into fabrics, stories and traditions. These were the original instructions for living given by the Great Mystery. There are stone tablets and scrolls with this information on it that have been buried and hidden away in many lands. They will be rediscovered and the teachings will speak again. The Medicine People of every nation were the first to work with Sacred Geometry. They used the symbols in ceremony and to contemplate the mysteries of the Universe. From these ceremonies, math, astronomy and language developed, but they are incomplete. There is much more to know about the Universal Mysteries, and this information is all hidden within the geometric symbols that we still use everyday. Remember.

DNA itself is Sacred Geometry. Look at the spiral of the double helix with diamond shapes stacked on top of each other forming a twisted ladder. This is the physical manifestation of the energetic diamond Vortex Ladder that carries the Spirit Essence from the Spirit World to the physical world and back again. Each of the strands that make up our personal twisted Vortex Ladder of DNA is composed of a string of geometric shapes that are encoded with bits of Universal Wisdom that helps us manifest the person that we chose to become and develop the gifts that we brought with us into the Earth Walk. These strings of geometric shapes, or DNA, are very intricate and complex. They hold the codes not only for our present life, but for knowing the past through our Ancestor's memories, all the way back to the formation of the Universe. They also hold the keys for the development of our species as the whole and complete beings that we were envisioned to be in the Great Mystery's dream. DNA is the physical manifestation of the code for remembering the Universal Dream and our individual role in it.

Each of the twelve strands of DNA has a special ability (or gift) and a shape, color and sound. Our First Ancestors carried a complete DNA, with all twelve strands fully functioning. The original human DNA carried the awakened geometric shapes that are the triggers for these gifts and abilities. Our First Ancestors knew how to use these gifts. They could communicate with the plants and animals. Much of what we know about medicinal plants, edible foods and survival skills were told to our First Ancestors by the plants and animals that shared their environment. Our First Ancestors knew many ways of healing that we do not remember, for they had the gift of intuitively knowing what was needed when situations arose. They were masters at regeneration, transportation and manifestation. They could travel anywhere as evidenced by similar carvings and symbols in many geographically diverse places.

Somewhere along the evolutionary line, some of these strands of DNA were disconnected. Most of us have lost the wisdom of these gifts, save a few indigenous wise people who still humbly display their talents in ceremonies and private healing practices. Now is the time for all humans to reawaken the geometric forms and learn how to use these gifts once again.

The Abilities of the Twelve Strands of DNA are:

1. Creativity- The ability to use our hands to create images envisioned in the mind.

2. Logic- The ability to create systems of ordered thinking and methods of reasoning.

3. Telepathy- The ability to transfer thoughts through nonverbal communication.

4. Prophecy- The ability to know what will most likely occur before it happens.

5. Manifestation- The ability to use thoughts to create physical objects and situations.

6. Healing- The ability to attain harmonious alignment between body, mind and spirit.

7. Empathy- The ability to feel what others think, feel and need through sharing their energy.

8. Regeneration- The ability to rebuild body parts when needed.

9. Teleportation- The ability to travel instantaneously to other locations and dimensions.

10. Transmutation- The ability to release physical form and change energetic form at will.

11. Fusion- The ability to merge your Spirit Essence with all life as one awareness of Wholeness.

12. Omniscient- The ability to know the story and wisdom of all worlds and dimensions within the Universe. The culmination of these gifts is for all of us to merge together to become the Great Mystery.

Creativity

Creativity and Logic are the abilities associated with the two strands of DNA that are fully awake within the cell structure of our bodies today. The strand of DNA connected to creativity carries the programs for the Genetic and Physical Structure of our body. The special gift of our human existence is to create. Humans have a unique way of creating, as we have been given hands with opposing thumbs that enable movements that most other creatures cannot duplicate. We can hold a pencil or paintbrush, make and use tools for various purposes, and use our hands to touch, shape, mold, weave, hold, express feelings and share love. We can see an image in our mind and then figure out how to make that image. Whenever the need arises, someone will always come up with an invention to make life easier or get a job done.

Another aspect of our creative gift is that we can create using focused thoughts. When we create something for someone else, or for a specific purpose, we can infuse that creation with love and good energy, thus the physical gift becomes a vessel for energy sharing. Geometric symbols can be shared as triggers imprinted in the energy of an object or activity given for exchange. Our Ancestors did everything with intention. They made every thought and action in the present moment with full consciousness. This kind of conscious creation enables sharing on every level of existence, making relationships complete.

Through our unique gift of creativity, humans have changed the Earth more than any other species living on this planet. From the time when our Ancestors first learned how to keep and use fire, to envisioning and building the wheel, to the development of present day technology, humans have expressed a myriad of creative abilities as our evolutionary awareness expanded. Just look around and you will realize the extent of our creative ability. We have taken the resource materials on this planet and molded them into our vision for living. The use of natural resources to manifest our creative ideas is now putting severe strain on our planetary environment. The Universe is infinitely abundant. Now our creative abilities must evolve so that abundance is shared rather than just consumed. The next step in using the gift of creativity encoded within our DNA is to manifest using focused thoughts to learn how to create what we envision through Unconditional Love, Universal Truth and Peace, and to share our gifts with All Our Relations and Mother Earth.

Logic

Logic is the ability associated with the second strand of DNA that is awake and functioning at the present time. This strand of DNA carries the programs for our Intelligence and Personality. Logic works with the development of thought and allows us to make order out of the world around us. Through logic, we separate observations and events into facts that enable us to understand who we are and why things work. Thus, logic analyzes everything we come into contact with. We base all relationships on what logic tells us. We make predictions on how things will work, how other creatures will act, how the seasons and cycles progress, and what the future will bring. Entire systems of thought—math, science, astrology, philosophy, language, and psychology—have been developed based on a logical understanding of the world around us.

Our Ancestors observed the world around them—the cycles of the sun and moon, the behavior of the plants, trees and animals—and then used the gift of logic to determine how everything came into existence. The creation stories were the first system of logical understanding. Ancient Medicine People developed logical thought through their understanding of vibration (sight and sound), math, astronomy and physical relationships. They were the musicians, artists and healers for the people. Medicine People also explored relationships and emotions and gave the people an example of how to live in harmony with the world around them.

Humans have used logic to create many systems of thought and institutions that have changed the Earth—education, religion, economics, politics, legal and social structures. Even though we think we know the true facts and the best ways of living, our development of logic is still very much incomplete. The gift of logic enables us to understand Universal Wisdom and Universal Law, but logic does not encompass the totality of Universal Wisdom and Universal Law. That means that we understand logic as it applies only in the Third Dimensional life on the physical plane. We still do not know the facts of logic that exist in other dimensions. I am sure some would argue that we also do not fully understand the facts of logic as it applies to our Third Dimensional existence and they are correct. Many people think our systems of logic are fail-proof but we will soon discover new facts that change our ways of scientific understanding, and we will see that all of our systems of logic will have to change as well.

The next step in using the gift of logic associated with our DNA is to develop intuitive wisdom and communication in order to know more about the creatures we share the Earth with, and to more fully understand the cycles of our planet and how the Universe works. More information will be revealed to us as we become adjusted to the Fifth Dimension. We will then be able to change our structures and institutions to support harmony and peace instead of separation and control. When we recognize that there is logic of the heart, which is Universal Law, we will expand our gift of mental logic to experience wholeness through aligning our body, mind and spirit. We must understand personal observations through the heart, learn inner communication, and listen to Spirit guidance in order to more fully develop the gift of logic encoded within our DNA.

Telepathy

It has taken four worlds for humans to evolve and develop the gifts associated with the first two strands of our DNA (Creativity and Logic). The rest of our latent strands of DNA will reconnect at different times as our energy shifts to accommodate the dimensional changes of evolution into the Fifth World, Sixth World and Seventh World. At this time, the gifts of Telepathy, Prophecy, Manifestation and Healing are simultaneously awakening as we enter the Fifth World.

Telepathy is communication through energy. The strand of DNA that carries telepathy programs our ability to Perceive Energy. At present, we are most familiar with communication through the spoken and written word in a system of language created through the mind. However, people who do healing work, those who spend a lot of time with animals, and psychics have learned to communicate through touching energy vibrations and interpreting their experiences within the heart.

When our First Ancestors came into the Earth Walk, an exchange of energy vibrations was the common form of communication. Old folk stories from every culture tell us about trees and animals that talk to people. Our First Ancestors learned how to live from the animals and found medicine plants and trees through energy communication with the actual plants and trees. They learned Earth's story from listening to the stones, water and wind. Because we share the Universal Energy Web, we too can remember the Language of Energy Vibrations.

Anything that has energy is alive in some dimension. Science tells us that a living being must eat, move, grow and breathe—however our Elders tell us that there are much older beings than humans on this planet, who live and grow in different ways. Stone People, for example, record the history of Mother Earth. They have been manifested in physical form for centuries and they move and change so slowly that we cannot perceive this process during our lifetime. The Stone People do have energy and this energy changes over time and circumstance. Everyone is at least unconsciously aware of the energy of the stones, as you can notice people flocking to the mountains during summer months and feeling very refreshed and revived when they leave. Children can hear the language of the stones, as a look into any small pocket will verify. Many healers use stones for their positive interaction with the client's physical and emotional. Both common and precious stones have been found adorning the art objects and artifacts of ancient peoples. Even the bible tells us about important breastplates made of precious stones. If you hold a stone in your hand and spend time with that stone often, you can learn about the energy of the stones and begin to understand energy communication. Water, clouds, wind, and the very soil under our feet are all living entities that are alive, with energy to share.

Before we can fully develop the gift of telepathy, we must become more aware of our Fine Lines and the energy connections we make with others. We must learn to honor the Sacred Space within others and ourselves. Using telepathy brings our personal secrets out into the open, so great love and compassion must be cultivated. Telepathy is a gift that must be understood within the context of family relations, because we are all one Earth Family. We must learn to treat all others as we ourselves wish to be treated under every possible circumstance. We must think with One Mind, love with One Heart, and embrace all others without prejudice as our sisters and brothers if we are to communicate with our energy in a good way.

Prophecy

Prophecy is another gift that is awakening as we enter the Fifth World. The strand of DNA that connects with the gift of prophecy carries the programming for Perceiving Relationships within time, space and location. Prophecy is the ability to know the most likely outcome of a situation before it occurs, based upon the present energy flow. Some of us are already developing this gift: for example knowing who is calling when the telephone rings; thinking of someone, and then receiving a call or letter from that person, or running into that person in town; meeting a person that you know will be influential; picking up a book or newspaper and reading something that changes your life; situations of perfect timing, synchronicity, etc.

As we become more perceptive of the energy that encompasses and animates all life, we become able to perceive individual thoughts. Thoughts create reality. That is to say, everything that we see around us was once a thought; from the inspiration of the inventor who designed the toaster that made your breakfast, to the thought of doing something thoughtful for someone, to the original dream of living in which the Great Mystery that created the matrix for all Universal Life.

Medicine People and seers of many nations were the ones who kept the gift of prophecy for the people and revealed their visions for the welfare of the nation and for the individuals who came seeking counsel. For example, Native Americans of North, Central and South America all had prophecies about the coming of the Europeans, so the arrival of early ships were stories that the people knew long before they finally appeared on the shores. Some Medicine People used stones or images to trigger the information while others used trance states. All of the prophets were consulted by the people and highly respected for their gift. Medicine People and many others today have developed the gift of prophecy to the point where they can give readings that affect the healing and choices of those who seek their counsel.

The First Ancestors of many nations foretold of the present time in their prophecies for Earth changes. They tell us that we are entering a New World where we can return to a way of living in harmony with the Earth and all the other creatures who share this planet. They also tell us of a planetary reconciliation and awakening in consciousness for the people, where our awareness will span many more dimensions than we presently know. All of the prophecies tell us that life as we now know it will be drastically changed. Some of the prophecies tell of planetary destruction and the disappearance of many species of life. Some of the destruction that the prophecies have revealed has already come to pass, however we still have the ability to change this story by changing our thoughts and energy. We can make choices to live in environmentally friendly ways, to make peaceful alliances with our human family, and to become responsible caretakers of the plants, trees and animals. The Ancient Ancestors recognized these choices when they included within the prophecies the need to return to the teachings of the Medicine Wheel and ways of living in harmony with the natural world.

If we are to develop our gift of prophecy to its highest potential, it is essential to understand the fluid nature of energy and the power of focused thought that originates in a heart backed by strong beliefs. We each must realize that we create the future through our present thoughts and then take responsibility for every one of our thoughts and actions. Mental discipline may be necessary to become the person that we envision: patience and love are needed to create the nations that we envision. We must take back the power to change our reality so that we are no longer stuck within the same recurring lessons or limited thought patterns. We are really all here on the Earth to live out one vision, that of the Universal Dream. When we release ourselves from emotions and personal expectations, and surrender to the evolution of the planet, the abundance of the Universe will flow freely for all creatures.

Prophecy must be understood as the revelation of one possibility on one path in a Universe filled with a million possibilities. As we become more spiritually mature, we will be able to see many possibilities for the future, make choices for manifesting, and then live out our personal visions as fully conscious beings. We must be prepared to use the gift of prophecy to bring alignment to our body, mind and spirit—and then work for the alignment of peace, harmony and Oneness for our planet.

Manifestation

The strand of DNA connected with the gift of manifestation carries the program for Magnetic Attraction. The gift of manifestation enables us to use focused thoughts to create objects and occurrences in the physical world. We know that the future is created from our present thoughts and many of us can already manifest what we envision, at least some of the time. However, in order to understand how the gift of manifestation works, we need to more fully understand the nature of the Universe. Scientists have proven what our most Ancient Ancestors intuitively knew: The Universe is simply energy vibrating at many different levels within the spectrum of existence. Some levels of energy are dense and slow moving, while other levels are light and traveling very fast. Many levels of energy vibrations make up the many dimensions of universal existence and include all of the thoughts, perceptions, and physical forms envisioned in the dream of living of the Great Mystery.

Energy is magnetic in nature, so it attracts other energy with similar vibrations. The dense energy bands exist in close proximity at one end of the universal spectrum and the light energy bands gravitate to the opposite end of the universal energy spectrum, with all of the other energy bands finding their places somewhere in between. When the vibration of a specific location changes, energy regroups so that similar vibrations continue to cling together. Our thoughts become the magnet that attracts energy to our life.

You have the ability to change everything about yourself simply by changing your thoughts and beliefs. We are creators. To fully develop the gift of manifestation that is encoded within our DNA, we must get to know our Spirit Essence, remember our purpose, and honor our connection in the Web of Life. We must flow with the rhythm of Universal Timing and trust that what we envision will manifest in the best possible way to perpetuate the Universal Dream. We must realize that every moment is a manifestation of our thoughts and keep our thoughts to those that perpetuate self-healing and harmonious relationships. We must take full responsibility for all of our thoughts and take action to honor All Our Relations, for what we manifest affects them as well. The next step in manifesting is for humans to link our thoughts together to create environmental balance and peace between all nations.

Healing

The strand of DNA that carries the gift of healing programs Vibrational Balance. We currently think of healing as making someone better. Our doctors and healers work with a variety of traditional and natural remedies and techniques in order to bring about an increased state of functional energy. However, this Fourth World definition of healing is extremely limited. As we evolve in the Fifth World, our definition of healing will expand to include being in harmony with all that is—embodying the essence of the Universal Dream.

Before each person comes into the Earth Walk, she or he chooses lessons to learn in a process of spiritual growth. Each person experiences lessons in their own unique way. We know that we can take energy into our Energy Web and it will affect our physical body, our thoughts, beliefs and emotions, and even our spiritual growth. How we receive energy is our chosen path for learning during this Earth Walk. Consciously or unconsciously, we each make this choice many times every day. Our purpose is linked with our individual Sacred Point of View and that includes walking through the lessons that teach us how to stay balanced. We know that we are not separate from everything around us. Keeping our awareness within this state of Oneness is what healing truly is, for then every part of our being will resonate with the vibration of the Universe that perpetuates life.

To eliminate the lessons is not the answer; rather the process of integrating our lessons creates the energy that restores healing and is essential for personal survival. Integrating energy means bringing energy into alignment with our personal vibration, thus nourishing our Spirit Essence as well as our physical body, thoughts, beliefs and emotions.

For many centuries, Indigenous Medicine People have been performing ceremonies to bring back the Spirit of a sick person. Through powerful songs, prayers and dances, they send out the call and Spirit responds, showing the Medicine Person a vision of what needs to be done to restore the balance between this sick person's body, mind and Spirit Essence. The Medicine Person then performs a sometimes symbolic, sometimes physical action to rid the body of imbalance and thus restore health. In some indigenous cultures of the world, this is still the primary way of healing.

Modern medicine has made great advancements in discovering how to repair broken and injured tissues, surgical techniques for maintaining heart function, organ transplants, and many other achievements. However, in order for true healing to occur, the patient must search outside the physical procedure to balance thoughts, energy and spirit. The process of experiencing an illness or injury is just as healing as the methods used to bring the body back into balance.

Fifth Dimensional medicine is truly holistic. Humans must first recognize that healing is a process of living, not just wisdom sought out when we are in crisis. When we remember that we all share the energy of the Great Energy Field, then we will make everyday choices to keep ourselves in balance through seeking situations that renew our personal energy vibration. Using our gift of manifestation, we must take responsibility for the state of our being and make conscious choices for change. We will learn to see and work with the healing geometric forms that are provided in unlimited quantity by the sun, moon, Earth and other universal bodies.

In the Fifth World, we will remember our connection with the world around us and honor the kinds of foods and medicines given by Mother Earth to our First Ancestors. People will learn to keep their energy balanced. We will be attracted to others carrying similar energy vibrations and will begin to form small groups, living, working and growing together, merging Energy Webs as clusters of similar vibration which intensifies the Energy Web of each individual member.

In order for the gift of healing to fully awaken in our DNA, we must realize that personal health is linked with the health of the planet. If we choose to work for a planetary sustaining ecology, we will perpetuate healing for all life. In the Fifth World, our gift of healing will be developed hand in hand with the gift of manifestation to balance body, mind, spirit, energy, relationships, the environment and the Web of Life, ultimately fulfilling the Great Mystery's Dream.

It will take a long time for us to fully understand and develop the Fifth Dimensional gifts of Telepathy, Prophecy, Manifestation and Healing. This is an exciting and very busy time in our evolution, for as we work to develop one of these gifts, the others also develop. Our awareness is beginning to perceive the full potential encoded within our DNA. A lot of conscious and unconscious awakening is happening within our DNA, personal awareness and relationships. Physical changes are occurring, restructuring our life to accommodate personal and planetary evolutionary changes. Our awareness is expanding, opening up new dimensions that provide a whole new look at reality and may lead us into entirely new directions. The awakening can be overwhelming at times, changing every aspect of our reality. Despite these rapid changes, we may feel more in tune at this time than ever before as our Spirit Essence shines with the memory of Great Mystery's Dream.

Our inner awakening is reflected in the world around us. Changes in the environment, social structure and ways of living are occurring in every country. We are breaking out of the old ways of thinking. People are emerging to act as role models and help set up a new paradigm. It is essential to honor our Spirit Essence and trust our inner voice. As the planet shifts and changes, our Spirit Essence will be the guide to help us follow Universal Wisdom and remember our purpose for being. Our Spirit Essence can help us understand our new perception and trust the process of expansion into the new dimension. The gifts of Telepathy, Prophecy, Manifestation and Healing must be fully developed before the next strands of DNA begin to awaken.

Empathy

In our evolution so far, our DNA has enabled us to understand the Universe through patterns of relationships and to create systems of living that express our thoughts and feelings. In the Fifth World, our DNA is awakening gifts that will expand our awareness and enable us to perceive in the dimensions of energy that exist beyond physical forms. The next level of DNA awakening will happen as we near the Sixth World. By that time in evolution, humans will be ready to join Energy Webs together into a single energy field. Our individual consciousness will reflect the multifaceted awareness of We.

The next strand of DNA to trigger on our journey to becoming a single planetary awareness is empathy, which programs Collective Awareness. Empathy—feeling what others are feeling—will awaken once we have fully developed the gift of healing. This ability goes beyond just an understanding of the concerns of others. In the Sixth World, we will learn to overlap our awareness with another person so that we perceive as they do and feel what they feel. While we are deeply sharing their perception, the other person will be sharing ours. At this stage, we will learn to merge Energy Webs with another person so that we can share the same Energy Web: the total of both Energy Webs that are much more than either Energy Web could ever be alone.

In order to develop the gift of empathy, we must completely let go of our fears and physical and emotional attachments. We must truly relate to others as reflections of our Spirit Essence and live in a place of total trust. During this process, we will learn to love within all the dimensions of our being which will bring a sense of fullness that we have never before experienced. The empathetic sharing of energy is a profound experience that will further progress the evolution of our species.

From there, we must merge our thought awareness and Energy Web with the planet—the plants, trees, animals, wind, water, and all of the elements and Spirits that exist on our world.

Regeneration

The next strand of DNA will awaken when we fully develop the gifts of healing and empathy. The strand of DNA connected with the gift of regeneration carries the programs for Holographic Memory. Regeneration—the ability to manifest physical body parts when needed—is based on a holograph of Universal Wholeness. We can only develop the gift of regeneration along with working to restore the environment of Earth, for we must have a healthy planet to support our newly developing physical, energetic and spiritual abilities. Our personal future is tied with the future of our planet within the very Vibrational Light Center of our being. Deep within our Vibrational Light Center, we hold the Great Mystery's Dream as the image of the holograph that will create what we need. All that is needed for regeneration to occur is for us to remember the details of the dream and desire to become the dream. The holograph will manifest in all dimensions for all beings.

At this point in evolution, we will be able to choose our physical lessons. There is no need for the resources of the planet to be depleted and polluted, or for entire species of plants and animals to suffer and become extinct. There is no need for humans to be starving, sick or suffer from injuries. Our lifespan will lengthen dramatically and we will choose the completion of our Earth Walk as a special passage surrounded by honoring circumstances. When we learn to take care of our planet as the caretakers that we were intended to be, we will discover the abundance all around us that is the key to regeneration on all levels.

Teleportation

Once we develop empathy and regeneration, the gift of teleportation will awaken. The strand of DNA that carries teleportation also programs Dimensional Expansion. Teleportation is the ability to move our physical body, awareness and Spirit Essence through time and space to visit other locations and time frames, both on this planet and dimension, and on other worlds or in other dimensions. By the time this strand of our DNA awakens in the Sixth World, we will have learned how to use our Energy Web. We will begin to develop new kinds of Fine Lines that will become personal pathways for traveling through the Earth's Energy Web. Our new Fine Lines will have the ability to carry our physical body and full conscious awareness to a new location where we can exist for as long as we wish. There will be no need for slow moving methods of transportation that deplete fossil fuels when we can travel in an instant using the gifts of our DNA.

Unlimited Trust is the foundation for using our gift of teleportation. We can only maintain a state of fluid energy through trusting in the process. As we learn to use teleportation on this planet, we will learn how to work with the Universal Energy Web (the Great Energy Field). We will create Fine Lines that will take us to other planets in our galaxy, and then to worlds beyond ours way out in the Universe. We will develop an unlimited awareness of the Universe and discover the secrets to universal phenomenon, such as black holes, which baffle our scientists today.

The idea of teleportation is not so far out as it seems. There are some indigenous Medicine People living today who can use this ability to travel to other locations or times where people have seen and spoken with them. The Star People who visit our planet most often arrive here using teleportation rather than on physical space ships. People who have encountered Star People can touch and communicate with them, usually in a nonverbal state of transferring information and awareness. When the gift of teleportation is fully developed, we will be able to travel through dimensions as far as our Fine Lines can take us. The next step in our evolution will be to harmonize our personal Energy Web with every creature in every world that we visit. Our Fine Lines will weave the Web of Life into a beautiful tapestry of wholeness in the Sixth World.

Transmutation

The gifts of DNA that will awaken during the Sixth World prepare us to merge our Energy Web together with the Universal Energy Web (the Great Energy Field). As we get closer to the Seventh World, we will trigger awake the next level of DNA. At that time, we will lose our physical form and merge Energy Webs together to become One Body, One Mind (awareness), and One Spirit Essence with our planet and then with the Universe. The first gift to awaken in the transition to the Seventh World is transmutation.

The strand of DNA that carries the gift of transmutation programs Geometric Memory. Transmutation is the ability to change shapes and take on new forms. By this time in our evolution, we will be experiencing life through our Energy Web. There will no longer be a need for physical forms. Our DNA will transmute into geometric forms encoding the blueprint for evolution within the Vibrational Light Center of our Energy Web. The secrets of life will become known, thus we can each experience any point of view that we choose. The gift of transmutation will allow us to shed our physical body and take on a whole new form of sensory perception. We can then fully blend into different forms—blending with another person or groups of people so completely that the blending becomes a new entity with a new awareness. We will probably spend some transition time blending together, then moving back into our personal awareness, and then blending into new forms with different people. Our conscious awareness will become intensified through this process. We will be on the verge of achieving what the human race has strived for through the entire duration of evolution—complete knowledge of Universal Wisdom and Wholeness of Being.

Transmutation is a gift that must be awakened by the entire species working together at the same time. To truly transmute, we each must blend with every other being, including the Elements and the planet itself. When the gift of transmutation is fully developed, we will finally evolve into our full potential as creators.

Fusion

The strand of DNA that carries fusion programs Wholeness. Once we have individually developed the gift of transmutation, we will blend with larger and larger groups to create many forms. At first, we will retain our individual awareness, but as the gift of fusion fully awakens within our DNA, everyone will take on the awareness of everything that is—Wholeness. Eventually all of the energy forms existing in the Seventh World will fuse into a shared Energy Web with a single awareness that is more expanded than all of the individual beings. All of the physical forms that have ever existed everywhere in the Universe will be part of this collective Energy Web. Each individual experience of living—including all thoughts, words, intentions, feelings and actions—will become one complete experience within the new collective Energy Web. Each Vibrational Light Center, Energy Center, Universal Wisdom Pathway, Earth Path, Truth Line, Memory Line, Fine Line and Spirit Essence on all of the worlds, in all galaxies and dimensions envisioned within the Great Mystery's Dream, will be part of the new collective Energy Web. This new collective Energy Web will become a new Universal Being: the Spirit Essence of the Great Energy Web.

Omniscience

The completion of the Seventh World will see all twelve strands of our DNA fully awakened. When the final strand of DNA is triggered awake, we will have completed the evolutionary journey of the Great Mystery's Dream. We will have fused our energy together with All Our Relations to become a new planetary Energy Web. We will then expand the planetary Energy Web to fuse with the Energy Webs of all of the suns, stars, planets and other universal beings of all other worlds. Our awareness will expand, intensify, illuminate and reenergize the Great Energy Field. A new Universal Energy Web will emerge as the template for a new state of being. Collectively, we will transcend body, mind and spirit to merge with the planet, the Universe, and finally the Great Mystery. All awareness will return to the Oneness from where it began, embodying Universal Law, Universal Wisdom and the entire dream for living created by the Great Mystery. The new being that we will become will be grander than we can ever imagine. The strand of DNA that carries omniscience programs the New Being that we will become.

Energy expands and extends into light.
People of energy light up the night.
Others awaken to their Light of Love
And listen to teachings from stars up above.

Transformation happens within every mind,
Creating thoughts of a New Humankind.
Within the Vortex, we embrace all possibilities
And grow beyond limitations with ease.

The Vortex gift comes as Mother Earth awakens,
Calling us to release old attitudes mistaken.
Now Walk your Talk, Walk your Thoughts,
And use the gifts that you have brought.

Diamond Vortex extends our energy family,
Calling Awakened Ones to join in Unity.
In the circle, we open energy channels to Earth.
In the Vortex, we send energy out for her rebirth.

Trust in the voices speaking from the Arc.
This wisdom will guide you through the dark.
Humankind is not alone—
The Universal Family welcomes you Home.

Grandmother Two Trees
and The Spirits Who Ride On The Winds

APPENDIX: ENERGY ALIGNMENT WITH HEALING TRIANGLES

Triangles can be configured to bring energy into alignment and open energy pathways within your physical body and between your physical body and Energy Web. The most important place in your body for anchoring triangular energy configurations is the pelvis.

The triangular shape of the pelvis balances the body and is the foundation for posture and movement. The pelvis sits on the Universal Wisdom Pathway and supports the skeleton, spinal cord and muscles in the physical body. Energy moving along the Truth Lines and through the Memory Lines is supported by the pelvis, which works together with the Vibrational Light Center in anchoring the Energy Web to the physical body. When you visualize energy moving in triangular forms, you reinforce the template of your physical body and the connection between body, mind and spirit.

Find a quiet, relaxed space in which to work with the healing triangles. Perhaps a few minutes of stretching or deep breathing will help you disconnect from your everyday schedule. Although some triangles can be done lying down, you can not effectively open up to universal energy in this position, as you are lying within the concentric energy bands of Mother Earth's Energy Web. It is best to do the triangles in all of the illustrated positions—lying, standing and sitting—because each position opens up a different direction of energy flow.

Read the instructions for one of the triangles. Visualize your energy connecting the three points of the triangle, and then visualize the area within the triangle filling up with bright light (you can use your healing color or healing sound). Infuse the area of the triangle with good energy (you can use a thought construct for manifesting, such as visualizing healthy organs functioning properly). Maintain straight posture and take regular, slow breaths while working with the triangles. Try to stay relaxed and keep your thoughts in the present moment. If you use a construct, keep your image clear and positive. If you find your thoughts wandering, be without judgment as you gently bring your attention back to the triangle.

△ △

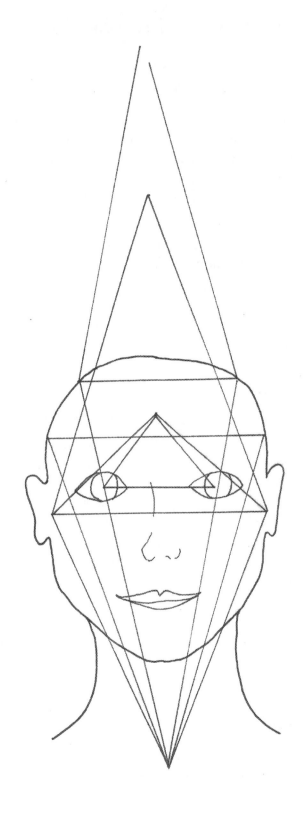

Triangles in Facial Front

The triangles in the facial front view connect Universal Wisdom within the physical body.

Universe, Two points on top of head- Opens awareness to Universal Wisdom within both hemispheres of the brain. Balances the Center of Universal Awareness.

Two points on top of head, Throat- Opens a clear channel for communication.

Third eye, Both eyes- Opens our vision to perceive beyond form. This triangle enables us to see with our inner eyes. Balances the Thought Center.

Third eye, Both ears- Opens up the ability to listen within. This triangle enables us to listen with our inner ears. Balances the Thought Center.

Both ears, Point beyond top of head in Energy Web- Develops the gift of listening beyond words to open up psychic perception and intuition. Balances the Thought Center.

Both Ears, Throat- Opens up communication through energy vibration as well as voice. Balances the Communication Center. *(When done together, the two "ear" triangles form a Vortex that actualizes Universal Wisdom and develops our gift of telepathy.)*

Both eyes, Throat- Enables the Truth to be seen and communicated. Opens inner awareness so we can understand what is not apparent, allowing us to perceive people and situations for what they really are. Balances the Communication Center.

Both temples, Throat- Balances perception with communication—our thoughts with our words. Balances our rhythm of receiving and giving.

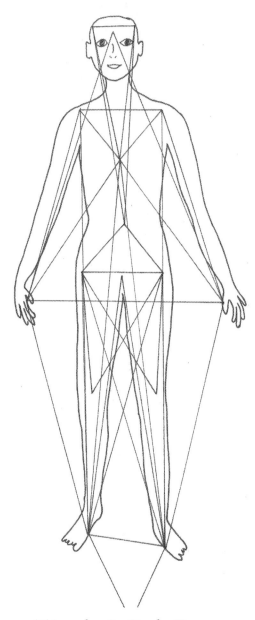

Triangles in Body Front

Triangles in the body front view are those that connect organs, joints, energy centers located just outside the physical body, and the places in the Energy Web where personal energy connects to the Earth and the Universe.

When this sequence of triangles is done in order, you will open up a personal multidimensional Vortex, extending the Vertical Vortex from the top of your head to below your feet. Your physical body becomes a conduit for energizing and replenishing the Earth energy, your own energy, and the energy of those you choose to share with.

<u>**Two points on top of head, Vibrational Light Center**</u>- Aligns personal rhythm with universal rhythm. Opens the Universal Wisdom Pathway. We bring Universal Wisdom into our mental and emotional bodies through this triangle.

(When done together, this triangle and Universe to Two Points on Top Of Head Triangle (from Triangles in Facial Front section) form a Vortex that helps us remember our part in the Universal Dream.)

Two points on top of head, Heart Center- Blends thoughts and feelings into a harmonious rhythm.

Third eye, Palms of both hands- Creates powerful energy for manifesting personal visions, healing, taking responsible action for peace, and helping others.

Both shoulder blades (in back), Pubic bone (in front)- Balances posture. Balances the spine and Universal Wisdom Pathway and keeps you centered with your awareness on the present moment. Balances the Vibrational Light Center (Center of Being).

Both shoulders (at ends of collar bone in front), Heart Center- Centers you within your personal rhythm, opens the flow of self-love and personal healing energy, and brings your awareness back into your heart.

Shoulder, Hand, Heart (Make a triangle on each side of the body)- On the left side, this triangle opens up pathways to bring energy into the body. On right side, this triangle opens up pathways for energy to leave the body. (When these two triangles are done together, they open up creative energy pathways to balance inspiration with action.)

Shoulder joint, Palm of hand, Sole of foot (Make a triangle on each side of the body)- Stand with feet squarely under your shoulders. This triangle grounds your intention with action.

Heart, Palm of hand, Sole of foot (Make a triangle on each side of the body)- Alignment of love energy. Grounds feelings.

Heart, Palms of both hands (Center of Doing)- Balances the Heart Center. Brings love into your actions, allows positive expression of feelings, and balances the receiving and giving sides of the body.

Both palms, Both feet, The Earth- This (five pointed) triangle balances your Center of Doing with your Center of Being. Balances the receiving and giving sides of the body. Makes an Earth Connection for your Universal Wisdom Pathway.

Reproductive Center, Soles of both feet - Aligns your physical body with your Earth Connection. Balances the Reproductive Center.

Vibrational Light Center, Both hip joints- Stabilizes your physical base, spine and posture. Opens energy flow between your Energy Web and physical body.

Both hip joints, Right knee/Both hip joints, Left knee- These two triangles align the Truth Lines to maintain straight body posture.

Both hip joints, Sole of right foot/Both hip joints, Sole of left foot- These two triangles work with the above triangles to align all the Truth Lines and maintain posture.

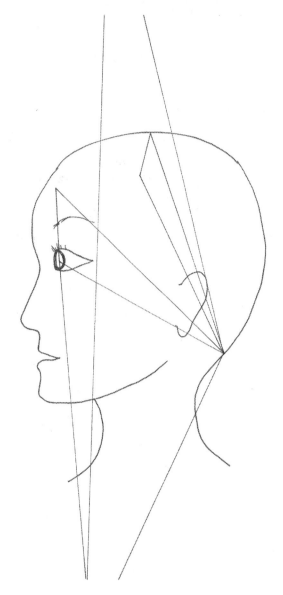

Triangles in Facial Profile

The triangles in facial profile intersect front to back inside the skull.

<u>Universe, Base of skull, Heart</u>- Balances the cerebellum with the heart and realigns our heartbeat with the rhythm of the Universe.

<u>Third eye, Sensory center on left side, Brain stem</u> *(deep inside the back of skull at the base)*/
<u>Third eye, Sensory center on right side, Brain stem</u> - These two triangles turn awareness inward to realign our Energy Web with our purpose of living. Balances Sensory Centers.

<u>Base of skull, Left eye, Heart/Base of skull, Right eye, Heart</u>- Balances feelings and perceptions to align with personal Truth.

<u>Two points on top of head, Base of skull</u>- Integrates Universal Energy and helps us understand Universal Wisdom. Balances magnetic and vibrational energy.

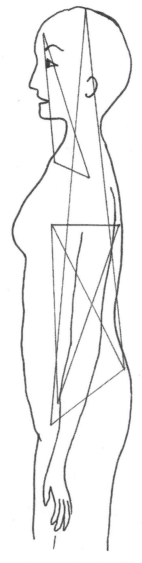

Triangles in Body Profile

The triangles in body profile show those that go through the body front to back, sometimes intersecting and energizing organs.

Top of head, Sacrum, Pubic bone (in front)- Integrates Universal rhythm with the rhythms of our personal cycles.

Third eye, Both shoulder blades- Aligns posture, expands the breath, and eases neck discomfort. Balances the Sensory Centers.

Heart, Vertebrae directly behind the heart, Reproductive Center- Balances the male/female energy within. Opens us up to self-love on a very deep level. Balances Center of Being (Vibrational Light Center). Brings feelings and actions into alignment.

Heart, Sacrum, Pubic bone (in front)- Aligns physical balance within posture and movement. Grounds energy. Eases sacral discomfort.

Triangles in Sitting Meditation Position

Looking from above, these triangles are formed within the body, front to back, to bring stability and strengthen Earth Connection.

Base of spine (tailbone), Both hip joints- Core triangle for body stability. Brings inner strength, focus and healing.

Base of spine (tailbone), Both knees- Forms a triangle of stability based on Earth Connection. This triangle relates to physical balance and flexibility, flexibility in times of stress and change, and balancing ourselves with the cycles of the Earth.

Two points on top of pelvis in back, Center of pubic bone in front- Balances physical and emotional energy within the body and is vital for maintaining an open conduit to replenish energy for ourselves and the Earth. Balances the Reproductive Center.

Center of Being (Vibrational Light Center), Open palms of both hands- Create this triangle and then allow the triangle to change into a double triangle (diamond) as the energy moves from the hands out to be shared with the Web of Life. This triangle harmonizes your energy and allows you to receive what you are ready to accept according to your present vibration. Balances the Vibrational Light Center, the Center of Being.

Looking from the front of the body in sitting meditation position, triangles are formed that allow manifestation to occur.

Universe, Both lungs- (Breath Triangle) Brings in the life energy of the Universe—the Sacred Breath of Life—creating a space for us to merge with the Great Energy Field. We bring Universal Wisdom into our physical body through the lungs.

Third eye, Open palms of both hands- (Awareness Triangle) You can use this triangle to increase self-awareness, listen for the answer to a question, or place a clear thought for manifestation. We bring Universal Wisdom into our awareness through our Thought Center. Balances the Thought Center.

Heart, Open palms of both hands- (Love Triangle) You can use this triangle to increase the love energy that you feel, for personal healing or to share energy with others. Use this triangle to envision your feelings as good actions. We manifest Unconditional Love through the Heart Center. Balances the Heart Center.

Looking from the back of the body in sitting meditation position, one triangle is created where universal energy enters the Universal Wisdom Pathway on top of the head with the base of the triangle at the location where your Universal Wisdom Pathway connects with the Earth. (This is true whether you are sitting on the Earth or on a floor inside.)

Top of head, Sitting bones (touching the floor)- Opens up the body as a conduit of energy exchange according to the rhythm of the Universe. Aligns and balances the Universal Wisdom Pathway.

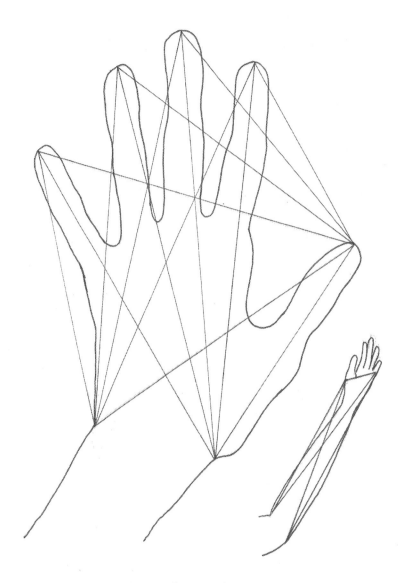

Triangles in the Hand

Hand triangles open up an energy flow for manifesting our intentions, and balance thoughts and actions within our body and Energy Web.

Elbow (both bones), Bone at base of thumb, Bone under little finger- Stabilizes energy flow with intention.

The rest of triangles on the hand are made through connections between the tips of the fingers and the joints of the wrist at the very base of the hand below the thumb and little finger. When we connect these triangles, we open up energy pathways in the hands for using creative tools and sharing energy with others. It is common to feel energy streaming out of the tips of your fingers after these exercises. Whether we share energy using our hands—such as Vortex Energy healing work—or if we carry out right actions to help others and promote peace, opening these triangles will assist with our work. When the sequence of hand triangles is done together on both hands, they open up our Creative Centers.

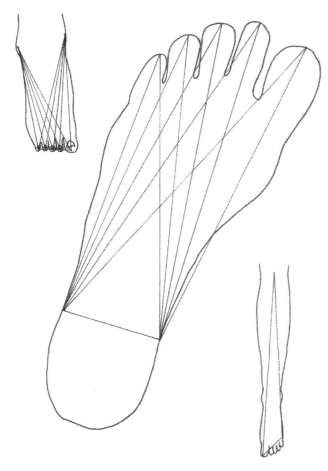

Triangles in the Foot

Foot triangles stabilize posture and keep us in the present moment with a thought of, "Be aware of where you stand and what is in front of you right now". These triangles open an Earth Connection, allowing us to make solid contact with every part of our being as we walk.

Knee, Big toe, Bone under small toe- Stabilizes our upright posture and balance.

Both ankle bones to each toe- Stabilizes legs and feet to bring physical, emotional, psychological and spiritual balance.

The joints of the metatarsals connect as triangles with the toes, ankles and points inside the Earth—both special Earth places that we have discovered and the locations where our Fine Line energy cords were anchored when we came into the Earth Walk. Configure your own triangular formations in the foot and learn about your Earth Connection. When this sequence of foot triangles is done together on both feet, the Grounding Centers open up.

The rest of the triangles on the foot are similar to the triangles on the hand, with all triangles connecting from the tips of toes to the bones on either side of the heels. These triangles ground us and form the basis for spiritual alignment and good posture. There are more triangles in the foot than illustrated here. These include connecting the reflexology and meridian points. If you have knowledge of these systems, it would be beneficial to create triangles to connect the points and notice what changes they bring for you.

Relationship Triangles

When you connect one of your Fine Lines with another person, or when they connect one of their Fine Lines with you, this process configures energy lines that can form triangles. Within these triangles, we hold our thoughts and expectations for future interactions that will occur between us. While sitting or standing in a meditative position, maybe after configuring your personal triangles, you can work with relationship triangles. Simply visualize your Fine Lines creating a triangle that connects you with one or more people. You can connect the triangle at the Heart Center or Vibrational Light Center of each person. Since a triangle needs three points to manifest, if you connect with only one person, you will need an anchor point, such as a location, a physical object meaningful to both, or a shared goal.

You can use a construct in the relationship triangle, but make sure that the image you hold within the triangle is positive for everyone involved and not manipulative in any way. I like to put love into my triangles, as the energy of love is always positive. If there is a conflict between another person and myself, love provides unconditional positive energy that affects both of us; thereby bringing a resolution that might not have occurred if I had attempted to visualize the resolution solely from my point of view. You can also put your healing colors or healing sounds into the relationship triangle to surround the relationship with harmony.

Triangles can be configured between geographic locations, cities, natural landmarks, rivers, oceans, mountains and other naturally occurring elements. If you take a map or globe and draw the triangles out, you will find unique relationships between locations. Our Ancestors were well aware of the energy held in various locations and left clues of their wisdom in the places where they built ancient cities. There are also relationships between the latitudes and longitudes of triangular connections between locations. Natural Earth changing events tend to occur in triangular configurations around the globe. When storm systems appear, draw relationship triangles to see how nature moves in triangular relationships. When traveling or making a decision to move, draw out the triangles on a map to see how your energy will be affected by the new location.

You can also plot triangles to connect energy between yourself and friends living in various locations. Many people who carry similar energy vibrations seem scattered all over the globe right now. We may wish that we could be closer to those we love because we miss having people around who really understand our energy. However, when you look at the larger triangular relationships, we are really each exactly where we are supposed to be, holding the triangular energy both on the planet's surface and anchoring it within the Earth. The relationships of the energy connections that we make, through our Fine Lines, our work, the location where we live, and what we chose to manifest in this Earth Walk, are beneficial to the planet as well.

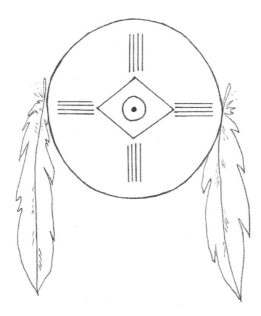

Spider is a ceremony leader with the Taino Caney Indian Spiritual Circle; a teacher of Medicine Wheel philosophy with the Planetary Wolf Clan Teaching Lodge; and an energy healer using Vortex Energy.

On her first Vision Quest, Spider was given the Vortex symbol and later taught by the Star People from Lyre to use the multidimensional Vortex and the Arcs to help align energy as the planet moves through the evolutionary shift. Spider has developed Vortex Energy into a system of exercises that can easily be used by those who are ready to shift awareness, and she has developed Vortex Energy healing sessions that have assisted many people with accelerating personal growth.

Energy is quickening and so is vibration. Thirty years later, the message of the Star People seems even more urgent. After passing through the 2012 Doorway, Spider was directed to share the teachings of Vortex Energy with as many people as possible. The Vortex is a tool that can help shift vibrations, personally and for the planet. The time to use it is now.

Spider lives in Western NY where she shares Vortex Energy healing sessions and personal readings using the Taino Glyphs, Animal Teachers and Medicine Wheel.

More information about Spider's Vortex Energy Healing work; Taino Glyphs, Animal Teachers and Medicine Wheel readings; and excerpts from other written works can be found on Spider's website: **www.spidersmedicine.com.**

Information about the Taino Caney Spiritual Circle can be found at
www.caneycircle.owlweb.org